Communicating Financial Management with Non-finance People

A manual for international development workers

John Cammack

PRACTICAL ACTION
Publishing

Practical Action Publishing Ltd
The Schumacher Centre
Bourton on Dunsmore, Rugby,
Warwickshire CV23 9QZ, UK
www.practicalactionpublishing.org

© John Cammack, 2012

ISBN 978 1 85339 732 5

A catalogue record for this book is available from the British Library.

The author has asserted his rights under the Copyright Designs and
Patents Act 1988 to be identified as author of this work.

Since 1974, Practical Action Publishing (formerly Intermediate
Technology Publications and ITDG Publishing) has published and
disseminated books and information in support of international
development work throughout the world. Practical Action
Publishing is a trading name of Practical Action Publishing Ltd
(Company Reg. No. 1159018), the wholly owned publishing
company of Practical Action. Practical Action Publishing trades
only in support of its parent charity objectives and any profits
are covenanted back to Practical Action (Charity Reg. No. 247257,
Group VAT Registration No. 880 9924 76).

Cover illustration: © Martha Hardy@GCI
Typeset by Bookcraft Limited, Stroud, Gloucestershire
Printed in the UK

Contents

Boxes

Figures

Tables

Acknowledgements

I acknowledge the contributions from many people in the preparation of this book. In particular I thank the Practical Action Publishing team: Toby Milner, Clare Tawney, and Liz Riley; and for prepress, Kim McSweeney at Bookcraft. Thanks also to those who have read and commented on earlier versions of the text: Simon Ager, Freda Cammack, Stephen Cammack, Gita Patel, Gopal Rao, and Tapiwa Samkange.

I am most grateful to those individuals and organizations that helped with the research and in many other ways: Richard Abraham, Simon Ager, Fredrick Ouko Alucheli, Caroline Ann Atieno, Felgona Atieno, Christine Babin, Thirtha Raj Bhatta, Saroj Bhusal, Janet Brubacher, Anne Marie Brundtland, Kibet Bunei, Josephine Carlsson, Ken Carlton, Sue Cavanna, Rachana Devkota, Samjhana Dhakal, Jyoti Dhital, Rebecca Didi, Eakraj Chhatkuli, Santosh Lami Chhne, Margarita Doneva, Judy Gachathi, Norman Gachoka, Gam Bahadur Gurung, Pratap Gurung, Bill Harper, Kate Holme, Jim Ingram, Elizabeth Kamau, Akjagul Karajakulova, Caroline Kariuki, Jivan K. C., Pramila K. C., Josiane Kielwasser, Ans Laver, John Lee, Noah Lusaka, Daniel Macharia, Raju Maharjan, Evelyn Mano, John Marangu, Mark Martin, Kennedy Mbuyah, Helen Mead, Lisa Mitoko, Dennis Mulenga, Jane Mung'oma, John Mwalagho, Florence Nodoro, Roseline Ngusa, Evelyn Obonyo, Fredrick Ochieng, Caroline Okang, Vincent Okello, Betty Okero, Paul Omondi, Erick Owino, Lily Oyare, Marion Pahlen, Patricia Paritau, Sanjay Patra, Waqas Pervaiz, Rama Pokhrel, Bhim Pokharel, Budhi Prasad Poudel, Arjun Pun, Bryan Rambharos, Gopal Rao, Sacha Rawlence, Grace Samkange, Rudo Samkange, Ratna Prasad Sapkota, Netra Pratap Sen, Suman Shakya, Bhim Prasad Sharma, Keshav Kumar Sharma, Buddi Kumar Shrestha, Mita Shrestha, Sachesh Silwal, Sajal Sthapit, Karuna Sagar Subedi, Prem Bahadur Thapa, Pushpa Raj Tiwari, Robby Vanrykel, Dolly Wanja, and Nigel Westwood.

Contributing organizations include: Accounting for International Development (Afid), Action Network for the Disabled (Andy), ALIN, ChildFund Kenya, Christian Aid, Civil Society Organization Network, Educational Resource Development Center Nepal (Erdcn), Financial Management Service Foundation India, Food for the Hungry Kenya, Forum for Rural Welfare and Agricultural Reform and Development (Forward Nepal), Environmental and Public Health Organization (Enpho), GVEP International, Kisumu Urban Apostolite Programme, Little Rock Inclusive ECD Centre, Local Initiatives for Biodiversity Research and Development (Li-Bird), Medair Switzerland, My Small Help, Omniglot. com, Oxfam GB, Sahamati, Save the Children Canada, St John Ambulance Kenya, Vétérinaires Sans Frontières Belgium, WaterAid, Women in the Fishing Industry Programme, and staff of the Practical Action offices in: Harare, Kathmandu, Kisumu, Nairobi, Narayanghat and Bharatpur, and Rugby.

John Cammack
Oxford, 2012

About the author

John Cammack works as an adviser and consultant, trainer, coach, and writer in the non-government organizations (NGO) sector. He was head of international finance at Oxfam GB and senior lecturer in accounting and financial management at Oxford Brookes University. He now works with a range of international development and relief agencies. His website is www.johncammack.net

His consultancy work includes: financial management and programme management reviews for European and Southern-based organizations, working with NGOs and community-based organizations (CBOs) to build their financial capacity, and advising organizations on becoming 'fit for funding'. His interactive training includes: financial management for non-specialists, training trainers (and specialist courses for training financial trainers), building financial capacity, and developing communication between finance and non-finance staff.

He is author of *Building Capacity through Financial Management* (Oxfam GB), *Basic Accounting for Small Groups* (Oxfam GB), and *Financial Management for Development* (Intrac). He co-authored Financial Management for Emergencies (www.fme-online.org). John is a professionally qualified accountant, manager, and teacher and specializes in the international not-for-profit sector. He holds an MSc in International Development Management, and an MBA.

Glossary of terms

Capacity-building. Strengthening individuals' abilities and skills within an organization to help it better achieve its objectives.

Communication. A way of transferring information, thoughts, and ideas between people. It is effective only if the sender and receiver understand the transfer in the same way.

Culture. 'The values, attitudes and behaviour in a given group of most of the people most of the time' (Munter, 1993).

Donor. An individual or institution providing funding and/ or other support to a not-for-profit organization. The donor may also be a not-for-profit organization.

Finance person. Someone who works with financial information and systems for most of their time.

Financial management. Using financial information, skills, and systems to control and make the best use of an organization's resources.

Financial statements (or annual financial statements). Summaries produced at the end of a financial year to show how an organization has done. Examples include: receipts and payments account, income and expenditure account (income statement), balance sheet, and statement of financial activities.

Facilitator. Someone who assists learning and discussion in a way that allows everyone to be involved in the process.

Funding. Money committed by a donor or organization to a programme of activities with social aims.

Management committee (or council, executive committee, governing body, or trustees). The group of people responsible for running a not-for-profit organization. Its members are usually volunteers who meet regularly to take policy decisions. In large organizations, members may represent the different aspects of the organization. In small organizations or groups, the management committee may be the whole organization meeting together.

Non-finance person. Someone who works with financial information and systems for some of their time.

Not-for-profit organization. An organization with social aims and objectives that is independent of government. Examples include: national and international NGOs, CBOs, and charities.

Partners. Two or more organizations working together for a common purpose. A donor is often one of the partners.

Programme(s). The activities by which a not-for-profit organization aims to achieve its stated objectives.

Stakeholders. Groups and individuals, inside or outside an organization, who have an interest in its well-being. They may include: partner organizations, community groups, service users, volunteers, staff, members of a management committee or trustees, national and local government, donors, suppliers, and the wider public.

Preface

This is a book about how to communicate financial information effectively. The underlying assumptions are that the reader wants to communicate well, and that by communicating financial information they can make sure that an organization's financial management capacity and programme impact are as effective as possible.

It is written for international, national and local not-for-profit organizations, NGOs, CBOs, and charities, although it is hoped that other people and sectors will also find its ideas and practical tools helpful. It is intended for finance and programme staff, chief executive officers, directors and managers, funders/donors, and fundraisers. Training facilitators, auditors, and members of management committees (trustees), and other non-finance staff will hopefully also find the contents useful. Indeed it is for anyone who needs to use or communicate financial information.

The book uses the terms 'finance' people to represent those who work with financial information and systems for most of their time; and 'non-finance' people to represent those who work with financial information and systems for only some of their time.

As a facilitator, consultant, and communicator of financial management I recognize that non-finance people need to have a working knowledge of financial skills so they can interpret information and systems in their work and in that of their partner and donor organizations. However I have come to realize that by itself this is not enough. Everyone who uses financial information and systems needs to *communicate* about financial management effectively. Cultural differences can make this process more complex, both within an organization and when working internationally. This book attempts to help individuals and organizations to develop these financial communication skills.

The international development sector is rightly concerned about the impact of its work with local communities. During my research the overwhelming response of those interviewed was that strong communication about financial management helps their programme activities to have a positive impact. In short, good finance means good development.

This book is written for, and with experience of, a wide range of not-for-profit organizations around the world. It offers practical tools and approaches that others have found useful. I am most grateful to all those who have shared their ideas through interviews, discussion, and participating in training courses. Much of the book is distilled from their wisdom.

Some of the suggested approaches may need to be adapted and developed further for different situations. I will consider the book to be complete if others provide further written materials adapted for their own context and culture. Please contact me if you want to discuss these possibilities and to be involved in the continuing research.

John Cammack

CHAPTER 1

Communication and financial management

This chapter identifies the connections between communication and financial management. It examines why communications in this area sometimes do not work. It also considers who we need to communicate with, what we need to communicate, and how we need to communicate the message better.

Why is communication about financial management important?

Much of the decision-making in not-for-profit organizations is based on financial information. Do we have enough funding to carry out our programme? Is our financial information good enough to take an informed decision? How can we attract new funders and maximize our income? Can we convince our donor that this activity is financially sustainable? What is the 'real cost' of what we are doing? What is its impact? Are we financially sustainable? Are our systems robust enough to prevent theft?

Good financial management communication can lead to:

- effective development programmes;
- more sustainable organizations;
- better financial management and funding;
- improved relationships with donors;
- a higher standard of reporting, for example to government, donors, and communities;
- informed decision-making, for example by the management committee;
- empowered staff who understand the financial implications of what they do;
- saving money by being cost-effective.

If the communication process has not been effective, the decision-makers will not understand fully the financial information and costly mistakes can be made. This is likely to affect longer-term credibility with donors, and the programme of activities will suffer.

Why is communication about financial management often difficult?

People who communicate about finance often say that others 'switch off' when they start to talk. Those who receive communication about finance often say that they are expected to understand obscure explanations of complex information.

Some financial terminology is indeed technical and there is a danger that the finance staff who give the information will use this jargon as a short cut to explain things. If I take my car to be serviced and the garage mechanic talks to me about the necessity to regularly check the wheel balance, I have no idea what they are talking about, and I am usually too embarrassed to ask what is meant by something so basic. However, this doesn't mean I can't drive the car away successfully. I don't need to know the technical words, but I do need to know that if I don't check the wheel balance my tyres will need replacing sooner rather than later!

At the garage, as in organizations, it is helpful if non-technical people are able to understand the basic ideas. I need to register for a basic course in car maintenance and non-finance people need to have a working knowledge of finance. It is also important that the technical person can recognize that not everyone knows, or needs to know, the details of what they do.

Communicating financial information freely, in a way that can be easily understood, does not always come naturally. Knowledge is often power, and people with knowledge are often afraid that 'if I tell you all I know, you will know as much as me and then you will no longer need me'. This approach can damage the organization and frustrate anyone trying to understand more. Managers need to use and reward good communication to encourage real sharing of knowledge and power.

Who do we need to communicate financial management to?

There is a wide range of stakeholders inside and outside any organization who all need to have clear financial management information. These include:

- Internally
  * members of management committees/governing bodies/trustees;
  * individual or organizational members ('the membership');
  * staff board and senior managers;
  * 'programme' and operations managers and staff;
  * fundraisers;
  * internal fundraising/campaigning groups;
  * other non-finance staff;
  * finance staff – professional and administrative;
  * internal auditors.

- Externally
  * partners, community groups, and service users;
  * donors – institutional and individuals;
  * national and local government;
  * regulatory bodies;
  * external auditors;
  * local and national media;
  * the public.

What do we communicate?

What we communicate depends on each relationship, or stakeholder, so we must choose carefully how much information is appropriate. As a general rule, those having day-to-day management responsibility (for example programme/operations managers) will need detailed information. Those taking a strategic view (for example management committees/donors) will benefit most from summarized information, with the option to ask for more if required. This may mean providing different financial documents for each group.

How do we communicate financial management information?

It is important to be able to communicate information that seems complex, in a simple way. To do this it is essential to make the communication appropriate to the audience, be it one person or many people. It is possible to understand the basics whatever your background.

We use a variety of methods to communicate financial management. Some include personal interaction: face-to-face conversations, telephone calls, meetings, training courses, and financial presentations. Others use written information: financial reports, instructions and procedures, email and its attachments, the internet, social networks, and letters.

The information needs to be: accurate, up to date, relevant and accessible for the audience, explained as part of the bigger organizational picture, and presented in a user-friendly and approachable way.

Support for effective communication

To support communication effectively we need an organizational atmosphere where:

- the culture of the organization shows the finance function is important;
- the director promotes and prioritizes financial issues;
- people regularly ask in meetings 'what are the financial implications of this?';
- information is freely shared and that is actively encouraged;
- money spent on upgrading financial systems is seen as an investment, not an expense;
- finance and non-finance staff meet informally;
- social events include both finance and non-finance staff.

Where finance people:

- are trained in communicating effectively;
- communicate without using technical words;

- have a positive attitude;
- are approachable;
- produce information that any user can understand;
- explain things simply and patiently;
- are seen as 'enablers' rather than 'police officers';
- are creative in designing the financial systems to be appropriate for unusual situations;
- learn about and understand non-financial work in the way others learn about finance.

And where non-finance people:

- see finance as a fundamental part of building an effective programme;
- are not afraid to ask finance people about things they don't understand;
- are willing to be trained in topics that they don't understand;
- spend time with finance people on a regular basis (for example, in joint meetings);
- pass on the skills they have learned to partners, other organizations, community groups, and individuals.

Finance communicators need to provide information to others in a way that they can understand. In other areas of life we sometimes talk about communication being 'centred' in a particular way, for example *student-centred communication* for education or *patient-centred communication* in health care. This suggests a way of communicating where the person giving the information does not just talk about the issue, but responds to the needs of other person in a step-by-step way, constantly being aware of what the student or the patient can take in. This way may take longer than just talking, but actual communication is more likely to happen as a result.

What we need with finance is something similar, although finding a particular phrase is perhaps less straightforward as the communication is with a range of stakeholders. We could perhaps talk in the not-for-profit sector, for example, about *user-centred communication* or *programme-centred communication* when talking about finance. Above all, the communicators need to be sensitive to people who find finance difficult and be able to help their understanding. Those who are trained in finance have to find a way of communicating that is underpinned by their knowledge, but using everyday language and not letting their training show.

CHAPTER 2

Building bridges between finance and non-finance people

This chapter examines the relationship between finance people, those who spend *most* of their working time with financial information and systems, and non-finance people, those who spend *some* of their working time with financial information and systems. It looks at their relationship and 'culture', and identifies techniques for improving their communication with each other.

Different approaches

We often think of cultural differences being between people of different nationalities. However, there can be cultural differences between people in different sectors (public, not-for-profit, or commercial) or organizations, or between departments or skill groups within an organization.

How individuals and groups see the world can be a result of their family, education, and training, their country of birth or settlement, as well as their experiences and the people they have met. No way is better than another, they are just different. If we want to communicate well it is important to recognize other people's cultural worldview.

There are cultural differences between finance and non-finance people. These two groups are rather broad, and both can include a wide range of skills, personalities (and cultures) within them. Finance people might include professional accountants who work in long-term planning, but also administrative staff dealing with routine finance work. Both may be dealing with non-finance people.

Similarly non-finance people can include those who understand finance, managing large budgets, who are financially literate and deal with complex operations. It might also include those who never work with financial information and are struggling to understand the basics.

People with the same skill or profession usually think about things in similar ways, and finance people are no exception. They can talk to each other using technical words as 'shorthand'. Being familiar with this jargon, it is easy to assume that everyone else knows it too. Of course, finance people are not the only ones to do this. Other specialized people in not-for-profit organizations can assume everyone knows their jargon. For example, the word 'mainstreaming' is often used by development professionals to mean a general issue that all parts of an organization's programme of activities focus on, such as the impact of climate change. Many finance, and indeed non-finance, people do not know what mainstreaming means.

Non-finance people sometimes say:

- Finance people do not understand our work.
- The staff speak in jargon.
- No one tests whether new finance staff can communicate well.
- I want someone to explain finance to me in a way I can understand.
- Finance is only for specialists.
- There's too much information.
- People in other cultures consider money differently to us.
- I visit our donors and partners in other countries and have some understanding of their culture.
- I was bad at maths at school so I can't do finance.
- The information is prepared for accountants, not managers.
- Just tell me how we are doing financially.
- They don't see it from my point of view.

Finance people sometimes say:

- Non-finance people don't produce accurate financial information.
- It is difficult to talk to them about finance without using some technical words.
- Non-finance staff are not recruited with finance skills and don't want to be trained.

- I keep explaining finance but they don't seem to understand.
- Unless everyone understands finance at a basic level, this organization will not succeed.
- There's not enough information.
- Why don't people in other countries do what I ask them?
- I'm working with people in other countries who I've never met.
- Finance is about technique more than maths.
- We need information that matches high accounting standards.
- When I tell you how we are doing financially, you don't seem to understand.
- They don't see it from my point of view.

These comments show very different cultures. Similar comments are sometimes used about other departments and individuals within an organization.

Alan Fowler (1997) identifies the relationship between finance and non-finance (operational) staff in international not-for-profit organizations:

> finance and administration bring a professional culture which emphasises adherence to a uniform set of rules; this culture is uncomfortable with the discretion, flexibility and continual variation which must be second nature to operational staff. In the worst case, conflict of culture leads to a 'them and us' mentality between development staff and administrators, accountants and auditors – at the cost of working for the common good.

There is evidence in my research (Cammack, 2005; see also Handy, 1985, for references to cultures) that people attracted to financial work and people attracted to non-financial work have different personality types. Finance culture often includes people who are logical and analytical. They like the familiarity of rules in systems and procedures. About 90 per cent of finance staff from not-for-profits interviewed in my research recognized themselves as belonging to this personality type.

Some non-finance people in not-for-profit programme departments said their main characteristics were: a wish to reduce the
'rules', and wanting more individual control and flexibility.
However, most non-finance people acknowledged that this is not
how it is in their organization. This seems at odds with finance
culture preference for rules and procedures. Non-finance staff
may also show elements of a finance culture, but my research
showed that this tends to be a lower proportion.

Around 80 per cent of those in both groups questioned
said they thought that these individual differences between
finance and non-finance people would affect departmental
or team approaches. This may explain the different attitudes of finance and non-finance departments towards the
importance of financial issues, which can lead to conflicting
approaches to dealing with and communicating about financial management.

These generalizations may be accurate but only explain a
certain amount. They need further analysis and breakdown.
For example, not all non-finance people in an organization
are the same. Individuals are likely to be from many different
professions and backgrounds, and have a wide variety of skills.
However, the generalizations help us see of why communication between them and finance people is not always easy.

How finance and non-finance people can communicate effectively

Our challenge is to break down some of the assumptions that
each group has about the other, address them, and find ways
to communicate effectively. If this is possible, the organization
and its programme activities will be stronger. Here are some
suggestions of how this can be done (see also Figure 2.1).

Management responsibilites

Senior staff member. For good communication, it is vital
that finance has clear support from senior management. In
particular, the senior manager must promote and prioritize the

Figure 2.1 Ways to achieve effective communication between finance and non-finance staff

financial side of the organization, by encouraging good relationships between the different staff groups and supporting managers in carrying out their financial tasks.

The senior staff member can often be the central person in talking with donors. It is important that they have a good working knowledge of financial management and inspire confidence that they can manage donor funding.

Other senior managers. It is important that the heads of each activity and department also have a working knowledge of finance and how it affects their work. Particularly important is that the head of finance is represented in the senior staff decision-making body, and that the finance view is represented clearly at the management committee (see also Chapter 7).

Build strong relationships. It is important that finance and non-finance staff work well together. In the not-for-profit sector, good working relationships need to be developed. For example, by involving both groups in writing funding proposals, reporting to donors, establishing clear budgets and financial controls, and in agreeing long-term plans. Introducing mentoring and coaching schemes can often improve these relationships. It can offer a way for senior staff to pass on good communication practice, through meeting regularly with a colleague, building their confidence through listening, questioning, and providing feedback (see Box 2.1).

Box 2.1 Relationship building

Practical Action encourages its finance staff to communicate effectively. Managers have invested a lot of time and effort in not only making the finance team as approachable as possible, but also helping them see themselves as part of the organization's programme activities. The finance team builds good relationships by:

- being sensitive to the needs of other team members, especially those from non-finance backgrounds;
- having an approachable attitude;
- being proactive about issues, rather than waiting for others to come to them, especially when working with people at a more senior level;
- talking in person to colleagues, rather than using emails. Email can be seen as harsh and impersonal, and are often misinterpreted. Practical Action has posters saying: 'Why use email when you can TALK TO YOUR BUDDY. Spoken words speak louder'.

The finance and programme teams work together to design project activities and put them into action, to tie work plans to budgets, as well as to report to donors. They are encouraged to see the bigger picture of what they are doing, and how their work contributes to it. A key part of this is making sure everyone knows what is happening in each other's work.

Source: Practical Action, Kenya

Employ the right level of staff for the organization. As organizations grow there may be an assumption that the same number and level of financial staff are sufficient. A small organization may cope well with a non-finance administrator keeping the records, and the director being responsible for financial management issues. However, as it grows, it needs professional advice from qualified accountants. This may include someone to manage the financial data (a financial accountant), and later someone to specifically provide managers with information about their programmes (a management accountant). Although this can be expensive, it is often more risky to go ahead without this advice. Growing organizations can bring in these skills, perhaps on a part-time basis. Sometimes donors will be willing to contribute to the cost of accounting staff.

Decision-making needs people with a professional finance background, but also with an understanding of the way the sector works. For example, an international development organization may support its partner even though it is financially weak. By doing this they help build the partner's financial capacity and make it more viable to deliver its programmes within their community.

Financial staff need to find creative ways to build their financial capacity, even though a purely commercial decision would be not to support the partner. Finance staff, especially those who are new to the not-for-profit sector, must respect the experience and advice of non-finance people in this area.

Interview and tests. When interviewing non-finance staff with financial responsibilities in their job description, set a test to show if they are financially competent. An example might be to interpret what is shown in the organization's 'budget and actual' report (see page 60). If the candidates need to work with a particular computer program, test the skills and knowledge required, perhaps by asking them to prepare a budget proposal for an activity on a computer spreadsheet.

When recruiting senior finance staff, during the selection process see if they can communicate effectively. Ask candidates to present a budget and actual report in a way that non-finance people can understand. Include a non-finance staff member on the interview panel to give feedback. These tests are only one way to help decide who to appoint. If candidates do not do well, it doesn't mean they will not be appointed. However, it does highlight the need for care in the decision, and to recognize further training and development needs.

Training for finance and non-finance staff. Make sure that all those who have any responsibility for finance as a part of their job description are trained appropriately. This applies to all stakeholders, including members of the management committee, staff, volunteers, and partner organizations. Financial management courses need to be especially targeted at the not-for-profit sector, and be presented in a way that empowers non-finance people.

Finance staff communicating finance to others may also need help. This book is a good starting point, and there are specialist training courses to improve their ability to communicate financial management (see also Chapter 8).

It is important to encourage finance staff to be proactive and take the initiative to work with non-finance people, rather than waiting for them to ask for help. In larger organizations, managers and departmental heads are in a good position to promote this.

Working together. In larger organizations, the use of interdepartmental teams can be an effective way of achieving results and also of building relationships by working together on issues that have financial implications.

In some organizations, more effort is made to learn about each other's work. This can be especially useful if staff are working directly with partner organizations and/or community groups where they need to offer them a range of skills. Using your own organization to learn from each other can be excellent training in financial skills, and allows staff to communicate this knowledge with others outside.

Where are the desks? If you are based in an office, it is useful to recognize where different individuals' or teams' desks are placed in relation to each other. Are the people you want to meet informally able to do this as part of their normal day? Ideally, finance and non-finance staff can interact at the photocopier or when they have a break.

Financial managers and staff responsibilities

How finance staff see themselves. It is interesting to ask a finance person or team: 'what is your role?' and 'how do you see your-selves?'. Some may see themselves as policing the organization, making sure that every financial rule is followed, while others may see themselves as supporters or enablers. This enabling approach can often achieve the finance and programme objectives by using the financial rules in a creative yet ethical way.

Neither being too rigid nor too flexible is desirable, particularly in situations where unusual events make the rules difficult to follow. Too much policing can limit how effective programme work can be, and too much enabling can mean that important financial rules may not be followed, which can result in a loss of funding and donor confidence.

The control/policing role is important, but non-finance people do not always see the real reason for policies and procedures. This needs to be patiently explained, in terms of helping the organization to work efficiently, and of following national and international standards of good practice. All organizations have policies and without them many donors would refuse to support them, so programmes would end.

Finding a way to support staff to balance these roles is the responsibility of senior management. Ideally finance staff should be able to see why it is necessary to adapt the rules (for example, the rule to obtain a receipt always may not be possible when travelling to small isolated communities) but still find ways to keep adequate control of the money. When programme staff also recognize why finance people need this control (for example, keeping receipts to be able to fully account to donors, who may not release the money without them), staff understand each other's needs.

Finance people can see themselves as taking sole responsibility for the organization's sustainability when there isn't enough money. They sometimes have to say 'no' if others in management are not prepared to do so. As a result, non-finance people can then think of finance as policing, especially if it is their idea that has been rejected! It is vital that finance people have the support of the director/senior management. Finance people need to explain the reason for each decision; otherwise good relations can easily be damaged.

Finance people must see themselves as part of the whole organization, and recognize that their role is not just about finance but about supporting and helping to build an effective programme for the organization.

'Internal marketing' of financial skills. How other people see finance can have an impact on how much finance staff can contribute to the organization and its programme effectiveness. If other staff see finance people as 'just keeping the records', they will not recognize the professional skills they can use to help the organization achieve its objectives. How finance staff are seen may depend on their professional background and ability, how they see themselves, their confidence, and how others see them.

There may be a need for some 'internal marketing' of the finance role. Managers who employ professional accounting staff need to talk with them about the organization's needs, what they are trained to do, and how they can help. They could include looking at longer-term planning and providing detailed information about costs and impact. Finance staff could also help to build the capacity of the organization and its partner groups.

Programme visits. Finance staff can often feel isolated in their work and disconnected from the more exciting programme activities. Visiting these activities for themselves can be inspiring, and help them to see how what they are doing relates to the wider programme work (see Box 2.2). They can also see how their financial skills could be used to develop the programme activities. These visits can offer an informal opportunity for programme staff to understand more about their colleagues' role in finance.

Box 2.2 Lisa's story

Lisa was appointed as a finance officer, with the duty, among others, to approve expenditure on programme work. ChildFund provided clear policies and procedures so that Lisa had all the guidance that she needed. She was happy to follow this and did her job well, asking for information to support and explain payments that she was asked to make. She saw her role as looking after the finances, with the programme work being done by specialists.

After about two years in the role, she had the chance to give a presentation to the coordinating committee in one of the programme areas and meet the people involved. Lisa visited their school programme and asked why the children were not yet going to school. She was told 'because the building isn't finished yet'.

Lisa realized that this was because of her delay in approving one of the payments, which didn't have the right supporting documents. Lisa started to think how this delay might have been avoided in a way that could have helped overcome the parents' and the programme team's frustrations, while still keeping to the spirit of the policies and procedures.

Back in her office she found a way to release the money quickly to complete the school. Lisa realized that waiting for the payment paperwork has consequences, and that her role was equally important to programme effectiveness as the role of programme staff.

This changed Lisa's approach for ever. Programme staff now sometimes tease Lisa that she is thinking like a programme officer, although they respect her objectivity and the way she talks about community issues. Her attitude has rubbed off on others in the finance team. People often comment on 'a great team spirit'. The finance manager respects Lisa for her well-balanced view of her work and the way she looks at the financial systems in an innovative and creative way.

Source: ChildFund, Kenya

Short, regular meetings. One-to-one meetings between finance and non-finance staff are an excellent way of building relationships and sharing knowledge (see Box 2.3). These meetings can focus on reviewing the latest budget reports, but they are also an opportunity to compare information, and for finance people to pass on some of their technical skills. It can also lead to finance people becoming involved in the programme meetings of non-finance staff.

Such meetings help finance people to better understand what their information means for the organization's activities. Their comments can add value to the programme and result in improved management information for senior managers, highlighting problems and opportunities in advance. When programmes are externally funded this can save money and often provide funds for additional activities.

Box 2.3 The meeting of programme and finance staff

Forward Nepal has worked hard to develop the relationship and communication between our finance and programme staff. We recognize it is important that this relationship works well, if we are to continue to receive external funding and enable our partners to develop their own capacity and skills.

We have achieved this strong relationship in four ways:

- **Staff orientation:** we make sure that new staff have a full orientation that includes the donor requirements, the application and reporting documents, and the need to explain and justify expenditure when travelling in remote areas when receipts are not always readily available.
- **Weekly meetings:** we conduct a brief weekly meeting of about an hour every Sunday at the head office. Activities conducted during the last week and activities planned for the week are shared among the staff in the meeting. This provides a picture to the staff of what is going on and how we should move in the coming week. Both the programme and financial matters are discussed in the meeting.
- **Monthly meetings:** our individual finance and programme officers meet to coincide with the production of the budget reports at the end of each month. This allows programme officers to assess what has happened, to ask questions, and provide explanations. It is an opportunity for finance staff to pass on some of their accounting skills, and for programme staff to explain more about the realities of their work.
- **Annual meetings:** these usually last about one to two days and bring together all the finance and programme staff to review each programme and plan for the future. Previous meetings have helped us identify where we need: budgeting improvements, more finance staff (which has sometimes resulted in obtaining additional funding from donors), or changes in administrative systems for working with partners. Generally a member of our executive board and a professional expert are present to bring in an external view.

Forward Nepal believes that its success depends on good communication. We follow all the communication approaches between staff: 'bottom-up', 'top-down', and 'horizontal'. The system of weekly meeting, monthly meeting, annual meeting, and other occasional meetings on a needs basis, helps the flow the information to the concerned staff, and the organization's members. These approaches create good relationships between co-workers and seniors. Timely discussion of problems and the generation of effective solutions in one forum help to make our organization vibrant.

Source: Forward Nepal, Nepal

Improvements to the systems and information. Organizations can improve their financial communication by working with the users of financial systems and information, and asking them what they need. By involving people in decisions they can help to create what is required, and are more likely to use the resulting information.

Those who don't recognize their lack of communication skills

People who feel they need to communicate better are often already well on the way to being excellent communicators. But those who manage a finance person or work in their team might be able to recognize a lack of communication skills amongst one or more of their colleagues.

This can be challenging for a manager. The finance person who lacks communication skills may well think they communicate perfectly – they think it is everyone else who is the problem because they simply don't understand. If asked, many non-finance people will say they don't understand what a certain member of the finance team is saying (sometimes all the finance team). Try asking non-finance staff in your organization for an honest opinion!

A manager's or colleague's role can be to try to break this cycle. There are a number of options:

- Consider yourself a role model: think about your own communication skills and review your strengths and weaknesses. Consider ways to develop your skills. Encourage good practice wherever it occurs. Try to model good practice, especially when you have meetings that include non-finance staff. Help colleagues to recognize their strengths and weaknesses, through conversations, meetings, and annual staff reviews.
- Ask staff to complete the 'Financial communication self-assessment' in Appendix A.
- Implement new ideas: this book has lots of suggestions for ways to improve communication. List those most suitable for your organization.
- Provide information about good financial communication.
- Talk with colleagues about their preferred way of learning. Some will say through written materials, others by listening to people, others by discussion, others by attending a course, others through websites. Find ways to help them in their preferred methods. This book provides lots of ideas for those who prefer written materials, and also gives topics for training and discussion – give copies to your staff.
- Provide training in how to communicate financial information effectively.
- Arrange a training session to help people to assess and improve their communication technique. This could be part of a regular meeting, or a specially designed course.
- Review job descriptions.
- If there is more than one person dealing with finance, identify who is the best communicator. Consider rearranging the tasks of each job to give each person the tasks that best suit their strengths.
- Recruit good communicators.
- Use interviews and tests to find good communicators (see page 13).

Explaining technical financial words

Finance staff need to minimize their use of technical words when explaining financial information to non-finance people or finance staff who are not professional accountants. If you use technical words, always make their meaning clear before using them. This not only applies to finance staff – anyone wanting to communicate effectively has to think carefully about the words they use.

The key to communicating finance in a clear way is starting from where the person's understanding is. Assume nothing, but realize people may already have some knowledge on which you can build.

Ask yourself whether a particular financial term is one that you or your organization calls by an unusual name or abbreviation, and see if there is an equally acceptable word that is easier to understand. For example, 'difference' is easier to understand than 'variance' for an underspend or overspend in the budget, although variance is widely used. Try to use descriptive words whenever possible. Some financial words however are so widely used that we just need to explain what they mean clearly.

When explaining technical topics:

- ask 'what do you already know about this topic?';
- explain where the topic fits into the bigger picture, for example, how managing money coming in and going out ('cash flow forecasting') helps the whole organization to be sustainable;
- be concise;
- link the topic to personal experience, for example, most people know about cash flow from their personal finances;
- avoid technical words and jargon;
- give simple examples;
- explain only what is essential for the audience;
- use pictures, diagrams, bar and pie charts, and other multimedia – not just words.

Specific technical financial words

When non-finance people (and some non-technical finance people too) are asked which technical words they find difficult to understand, they are likely to have a long list. Perhaps the most frequent suggestions are 'accruals and prepayments' and 'depreciation'. It is important that finance people can explain such words in a way that others can easily understand.

A non-technical description of these and other financial words is shown in Appendix B.

CHAPTER 3

Communicating cross-culturally

The focus of this chapter is how to communicate when working with different international cultures. You do not have to travel to do this as many of the places where we live and work are made up of many cultures. We may also communicate with people from different cultures by telephone and the internet without ever leaving our place of work. This chapter looks at ways to understand cultural differences and how to improve our communication about finance between cultures.

The cultural differences between finance and non-finance people, discussed in the previous chapter, become more complex in organizations that work internationally. Communication can involve different ways of looking at the world. The common language used for communication may not be either person's first language.

Andreas Fuglesang (1982) quotes an elderly village woman in Zambia (Mukahamubwatu), who puts it like this: 'You people do not understand (that) your words do not belong to our minds'.

You may have a similar experience to this with communication of your own. This experience can apply as much to communication about finance as to any other topic of conversation.

International cultures: 'High-context' and 'low-context'

Adding different national or regional cultural influences can make clear communication more difficult because each culture may look at financial issues in a different way. Edward T. Hall (1989) identifies 'high-context' and 'low-context' cultures to explain why people in different countries and societies communicate differently.

Although this is a generalized approach and no culture is exclusively one or the other, Hall argues that most cultures tend towards being high- or low-context. His approach helps us to identify why things are not always what we expect when we look from another person's cultural viewpoint. The terms are probably most useful to help us understand particular situations, rather than whole societies of people. Some key differences are listed in Table 3.1.

People from a low-context culture, can experience high-context with their families, close friends, and in social groups. Much of the communication then can be by a look or the individuals' knowledge of what is happening. This can be difficult for an outsider to this culture who does not share or understand it.

Perhaps when someone meets his/her prospective spouse or partner's family for the first time, they might be entering a high-context (family) culture, which may be quite different from their previous experience. It may take time before the new person fully understands this culture.

Table 3.1 Aspects of high- and low-context cultures

High-context cultures	Low-context cultures
Socialize and establish relationships and trust first, then go to business	Start with the business and focus on the task, relationships may come later
Tend towards indirectness; people often imply and suggest	Tend towards directness; people are explicit
Multiple connections and people understand each other intuitively	More independent with fewer shared experiences
Goal is preserving and strengthening the relationship, always try to 'save face'	Goal is to complete tasks by receiving and giving clear information
Less written and formal information available, more verbal communication	Knowledge and information more accessible and transferable; more written communication
May say 'yes' or sometimes nothing at all as a polite way of saying 'no'	Say 'yes' and 'no' to mean what they say
Don't always need to use words, people intuitively understand	Say things clearly, and people do not imply what is meant
There is always more time and deadlines are flexible	Time is limited and deadlines are fixed

Someone from a high-context culture can experience a low-context culture at an airport or large shop, where information is clearly shown but where there is no one to answer questions. A visitor to such a culture may feel more comfortable talking to a real person than using the information on display. Low-context cultures are sometimes easier to enter because they provide information and don't rely on building a relationship. However this culture too can be based on rules that are difficult to learn quickly. A summary of high-context culture could be: 'maintain relationships at all costs'. A low-context summary is: 'be direct and say what you mean'. These are quite different ways of seeing things.

A number of writers suggest that people brought up in or from a family with a culture from Africa, Eastern Europe, the Middle East, South America, South Asia, Southeast Asia, and Southern Europe tend towards high-context culture. Those from Australasia, North America, and Northern Europe tend towards low-context culture.

Of course these contexts are a generalization, and relate to the culture as a whole rather than all the individuals within that culture. Both high- and low-context people exist in every culture, and many people use aspects of both cultures in everyday life.

In addition almost all countries/regions of countries now include people who do not see themselves as part of the dominant national/regional culture. This provides a great richness of diversity, and opportunities to learn. It also means that it is helpful to find out about other cultures to help us communicate better, wherever we live and work. Think about your own culture, and others you may know, and the differences and opportunities that exist in your local community, town, and country.

Crossing cultures in everyday communication

The simplified distinction between high- and low-context cultures affects organizations and individuals. Cultural differences start to explain why communication, including financial management communication, is not always what it seems.

Below are some examples of when our cultural experience can mean we interpret a situation differently. The explanations given of high- and low-context cultures are at two ends of a spectrum. There are of course variations in between. As you read through each one, try to identify where your culture would place itself, and where you consider yourself to be. Think where people from other cultures you interact with would place themselves (if you have a good relationship, ask them!).

Directness and indirectness

This refers to the level at which to address an issue with someone, balancing caring for the relationship with making it very clear what you mean. High-context: people suggest or imply what they mean, and are cautious in saying exactly how things are in case it upsets the other person. Low-context: people say exactly what they are thinking and mean, and there is no need to interpret.

An example. A funder says some of the receipts and invoices the administrator sent are missing. The funder wants to know where they are, and asks for them to be sent immediately. The administrator had known the funder would want the receipts, but programme staff had not been able to obtain them while travelling in a remote area. The administrator doesn't want to upset the funder by saying they were not available and so never replies.

Techniques to use. Unless you know the recipient of your communication very well, don't presume you know how they will react. Think about the cultural aspects and be ready to adapt your communication style to be more direct or indirect. Try not to be upset when people are direct with you ('they seem aggressive'), or indirect with you ('why don't they just say what they mean'). If working with a high-context culture be aware of what is written/said and not said. Try to look for what is implied as well as what is said. Be more tactful. If working with a low-context culture, accept what is written/said as being what is really meant. Be more concise.

'Face saving'

This is the extent to which people feel 'put down', criticized, or embarrassed, and how you communicate to avoid any damage to someone's self-image. High-context: maintaining the relationship is the main aim. If what you are about to write or say may damage the relationship, then change the words. Instead write or say what the other person would like to hear, but try to keep the meaning. Low-context: explaining things accurately is more important than avoiding upsetting someone. It is all right to say 'no' and confront people. Receiving and giving consistent information is the main aim.

An example. The accountant criticizes his administrator by email for the figures she sent, which are incorrect and were received after the deadline. He copies the email to the administrator's manager and to the coordination office, saying 'why couldn't she tell me what was wrong and that there would be a delay?'. After this incident the accountant notices their relationship grows worse. The administrator's previously friendly emails start to become less frequent and quite short. Soon after that the accountant hears that she has left the organization; someone says she was very upset with him.

Techniques to use to help someone save face. If someone has made a mistake, help them to back down gracefully. Always try to provide people with a way to explain things rather than using words that push them into a corner from which they can't escape. Avoid disagreement and criticism in front of others, and use it cautiously in all situations.

'Power distance'

This is the way in which power, authority, and status are distributed in an organization. High-power distance: power is kept with the most senior person and staff defer to them. Managers decide how much authority to delegate. It would be disrespectful to question the views of your manager. Everyone has their rightful place. Low-power distance: manager shares power with staff. Staff are given general instructions but then expected to carry out their job with minimal supervision. They are likely to make their own decisions, be consulted about decisions, and asked for their views. Relationships between staff tend to be informal. Inequalities between people should be minimized.

An example. An international finance director goes to meetings with an international office team. She wants to develop ideas on the proposed way of working with financial reporting. She explains the system in detail and invites comments from everyone and says it's only ideas at the moment and anything can still be changed. Everyone nods when she asks if it looks all right and what could be improved. No one other than the country director says anything. The international finance director wonders why the group does not seem interested in a scheme that would change their way of working. When she had given a similar presentation in her home office people came up with lots of ideas.

Techniques to use.   Be aware of the power distance and adjust your communication style as needed. Be polite. If working with high-power distance, give clear instructions and expect the need to give support. Respect age and status. If working with low-power distance, involve people in decision-making, expect people to take the initiative, be prepared to be less formal.

Time and deadlines

This refers to the use of different approaches to time. High-context: time is flexible enough to fit around people. Deadlines can be extended. The aim is to appreciate the time we have. Low-context: time is limited. People are less important than time. Deadlines are important and not easily changed. The aim is to complete tasks within a specified time.

An example.   When our donor's head of finance is visiting our office, we arrange everything just as he requested. He told us the people he wanted to see and when the meetings should take place. Everyone is available to meet him just as he requested. When our head of finance is due to visit the donor's office, he also says who he wants to meet and when, but during the visit he isn't able to meet many of the people because they are either not there or too busy.

Techniques to use. Be aware that other people may see time differently. If working with someone from a low-context culture, contact them to meet or agree a deadline well in advance. When they have agreed this, it is unlikely to change. The person will usually let you know if they need to change anything. If it becomes difficult or impossible for you, let them know as soon as you can and explain the reason. If you are working with someone from a high-context culture and you fix a deadline, explain why this deadline is important and if possible build in a little extra time. If a deadline or appointment has been arranged in advance, check that it is still possible sometime before. You need to be flexible too.

Attitudes to risk

This is the willingness of different cultures to attempt new things. This can also be affected by an individual's personality. Non-risk takers: people do not take risks and like rules to explain how to do things. If something new is tried and goes wrong, they fear they will take the blame. Risk-takers: people will take risks, even though the outcome may not be known. It is seen as a way of learning. For them it is all right to try and fail, and they don't fear they will be blamed if it goes wrong.

An example. During a week-long course to train financial trainers to work with partners, the facilitator asks different groups for a brief review of the topics covered at the end of each day. The first day someone describes what happened session by session. The facilitator thinks it needs to be livelier, so at the beginning of the second day spends time suggesting ways that the group could present the review using audio-visual aids, doing interviews, or even playing a game. She brings in lots of colourful materials that the groups can use. Everyone seems excited and keen to try out the ideas and the facilitator is looking forward to the second review, but the group again just describes what happened. None of the new training ideas are tried. The facilitator goes away wondering why the group had seemed enthusiastic but not used any of the ideas.

Techniques to use. Recognize the level of risk that an individual is able to take. If this is high, encourage colleagues to try new things and learn to benefit themselves and the organization. If the level is low, respect this and encourage small new steps, but only when you fully support them with clear explanations of what is required. For both groups, avoid blaming when things go wrong, and celebrate what goes well and the learning that occurs.

Ways to improve cross-cultural financial communication

It is important to understand how our cultural background affects our style of communication. From this we are able to learn from each other about how to communicate better (see Figure 3.1). Within every culture and context individuals will be different, so it is hard to say what will work in every situation. Here are some approaches that can work to improve communication across cultures. Try, use and adapt them for yourself.

Finding out

Recognize the difference. Recognize that there may be differences in the way you and the person you are communicating with understand the world. Observe how the other person responds to your communication and try to work out what is happening. Use Hall's high-context and low-context culture ideas as a starting point to know how direct you should be.

Find out about the culture. If working internationally, take time to learn about the culture of the people you are communicating

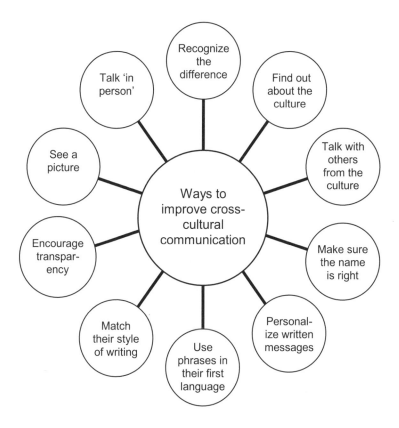

Figure 3.1 Ways to improve cross-cultural communication

with. Read what you can and, if possible, meet other people from the culture and get to know them. But remember that not everyone from the culture will be the same, and there are many subtle variations in every culture.

Talk with others from the culture about their approach.   When you have developed a good level of trust, ask the person you are communicating with how they approach work topics. Start with some easy questions. Try to discover what similar values and experiences you share. Acknowledge and value what they tell you. If you have only been in contact by letter or electronically, if possible try to meet face-to-face. This can significantly improve the relationship. It is an opportunity to listen and learn. You can then ask them questions and experience their culture yourself. People are usually eager to tell you about their culture.

Make sure the name is right. Names are important to all of us, and communication is more effective if we use the right name, correctly spelt. If using email, the way someone signs the message can be an indication of what they want to be called. If there are accents or unfamiliar letters in the name, copy and paste it when you reply to make sure it's exactly right.

Different cultures can put the family name(s) and given name(s) in a different order. The family name may come first, middle, or last. Whether speaking or writing, a title such as Mr or Ms may be used before either the given or family name or both. Take care that the name and spelling are always exactly right. If in doubt ask the person 'what should I call you?', and find a way to remember for future use. If possible ask the person to write their name down for you.

Good communication at a distance

Personalize written messages. If communicating at a distance, most people appreciate something personal before starting with the business, especially in high-context cultures, for example, 'hope all is well with you and your family' or 'how are you?'. Always treat people as individuals and with respect. If you are writing to someone in low-context cultures, you may want to concentrate only on the business, so adapt to their style, and be brief with the personal part.

Learn/use phrases from the other person's language. Often communication across cultures has to be in a language that may not be the first language of either the sender or receiver. If so, most people appreciate it if you try to go beyond it, even a little. Just 'hello' or 'how are you?' in the recipient's first language recognizes that they speak differently most of the time.

These phrases should not be over-used and perhaps one or two phrases each time you communicate are enough. As far as you can, make sure that you have the right language for the person you are communicating with. Many countries use a variety of languages. If you are in doubt ask 'which language do you speak?' or ask other colleagues. This applies to face-to-face meetings as well. There is a list of some phrases in a selection of languages in Appendix C (see also Box 3.1).

Box 3.1 Communication between cultures

We are an organization based in South Asia and work with partner organizations in Bangladesh, India, Nepal, Sri Lanka and Tibet. Whilst working with people in a variety of countries we have had to learn how to relate to, and communicate with, people in their own culture. Finance and programme staff often visit partners together. This is helpful because one of them has usually met the partner's staff, and this improves relationships immediately. It has been found that communication works well by:

- being open, friendly and transparent;
- using greetings and other words in the partner's own language to reassure them and show respect for them;
- having someone who knows both parties (maybe a staff member who has been there for a while) to make introductions on the first visit, or to make the introduction through the first email message;
- reflecting the style of the other person in email messages, for example, how they address the person, how direct or indirect they are, and how formal or informal. When they write, use similar words to them, and similar length of sentences;
- encouraging the other person and not being critical

The organization has found that working like this improves relationships between staff and those of our partners in all parts of both organizations – fundraising, programme, and finance and administration. It has also found that this style of communication works well with donors, giving them confidence in the organization and its work. Having good relationships is important when applying for further funding and to make sure our programme is effective.

Source: From research with an organization in Asia

Match the style. Write to the person in the same way that they write to you. If they say 'hi' do the same, but if they are more formal, be formal too. Also try to use similar phrases and words. Communication improves as we hear/see familiar words used.

Encourage transparency. In the international not-for-profit sector, being open, clear, and understandable, sometimes called 'transparency', is very important and is a generally accepted way of working, especially about financial issues. However this may be different from an organization's way of working that does not usually share information freely.

Sharing information within and between partner organizations is considered good practice for not-for profit organizations. Try to make information readily available, for example, by putting the annual financial statements and other financial details on your website and sending copies of the statements to all stakeholders. This gives stakeholders, and particularly donors, the assurance that you have nothing to hide. Many donors accept that organizations make mistakes, so occasional errors should not be a reason for not being open. It is generally better for you to tell the donor rather than for them to find out from someone else. If donors find a 'perfect' organization, they would be likely to say that there is 'no reason to fund them!

See a picture. If you communicate regularly with someone you have not met, it is useful to see what each other looks like. Having a visual image can improve communication, but think about any misunderstandings of the request. Be careful if you are of different genders, and respect the fact that someone might cover their face at work. Wait until you have built up some trust before asking. You could perhaps ask if they want to join your social networking site and see a picture there. An alternative is to ask someone else who may visit if they have a photograph, or to take one either of the individual or the team next time they meet. You may like to arrange a visual image for everyone in the organization.

Talk to each other in person. If you usually communicate by email, it is helpful to talk to the other person occasionally, even if they are the other side of the world. Internet telephone systems make this possible at little or no cost. With webcams it is even possible to see each other. Communication and relationships can improve considerably through this kind of contact and it is often more effective in high-context cultures.

For large organizations, consider bringing the international or regional finance and/or other staff together for a workshop to think about common issues. Much improved communication and learning can happen from these events. It can be expensive but talk with donors about possible funding.

Message content

Asking for information. Be courteous and polite when asking for something. Be specific about what you need and keep communications short. If possible, avoid a long list of questions, but instead concentrate on two or three important items – it is useful to number each point for clarity.

Use open questions, such as 'how', 'what', 'where', 'who', 'why', and 'when', rather than those requiring just a 'yes' or 'no' answer. For example, if you ask 'do you have any comments on the budget report?' the answer may well be 'no'. If you ask 'what comments do you have on the budget report?' or 'what else do you need to know about the budget?', you are more likely to receive a detailed reply. Consult people about the way forward rather than suggesting all the answers yourself.

Negotiate deadlines, and don't assume that the other person will think about deadlines in the same way as you. State the reason for the deadline, for example, 'the papers for the management committee need to be sent out by 12 June, so I need your report by 10 June'. Always send a note of appreciation when other people respond – even if they are little late. If a deadline cannot be met, inform everyone affected as soon as you can, and explain the reason why. Be willing to renegotiate a new date.

Think about the use of words. When you are not communicating in the first language of the person receiving the message, keep the communication clear and simple. Try to:

- Avoid slang – words used in one country that are not likely to be known elsewhere.
- Avoid idioms – a way of saying when the meaning is not obvious from the words used. For example 'I want the report by yesterday' means you want it as soon as possible, not literally by yesterday, which is impossible! If you use idioms expect other people to be confused.
- Avoid metaphors – for example sporting expressions such as 'it hit me for six', for which you need to understand the rules of cricket!
- Avoid words with different meanings – words such as 'summer' and 'winter', which are not at the same time of year in other parts of the world. Think about the way the other person would understand it.
- Avoid complicated sentences – for example, 'if you send me the report, and make sure it is not too long, but send it quickly so that I can comment on it and give it to the director before she leaves on Friday and then she can take the content with her when she travels'. Instead, use short and clear sentences.
- Be specific where possible – rather than saying 'I'll give you a ring tomorrow', which is general; say 'I will telephone you on Thursday at 10 a.m. your time'.

Use plain language wherever you can (see Chapter 5). If the other person is not a fluent speaker of your language, they are also likely to struggle with any long or technical words, and words used in an unusual setting. They may be a little embarrassed to admit that they don't understand. If you have to use complicated words, make sure they can be checked in a dictionary.

Avoid criticism and be careful with praise.   No one likes to be criticized, but in some cultures it is completely unacceptable to talk about someone's faults in public or in a shared email. It could result in a 'loss of face' (see page 27), reputation, and possibly be an end to the relationship. If you must say something that could be seen as negative, try to include it between more positive comments before and after, and think carefully about how you write or say it.

In some cultures, public praise is welcomed, but in others it might be seen as an insult: 'So you mean I wasn't doing this well before?'. Be encouraging, but check what is culturally acceptable first.

Think about the audience. If circulating information to a large group, think about how the different readers will receive your communication. Try to prepare the communication for the different audiences. This may take slightly longer but it will make your communication more effective.

Be aware, be yourself, and don't worry. Although you need to be aware of cultural differences and be as well informed as possible, don't worry too much about getting it wrong. Learning is often achieved through making mistakes, so try to learn from your own and others' mistakes. Most people recognize that foreigners make mistakes and are not quick to judge. A common phrase people use is: 'It's all right, they're not from round here!'.

Above all be yourself and enjoy the wonderfully varied experiences that different cultures bring. Being open, sincere, and willing to learn and adapt will mean others accept you more quickly.

Organizational, professional, and sector cultures

Organizations have their own cultures. This can be different from the dominant national culture where they are based. If this organizational culture is strong, staff may adopt it at work, even though it contradicts the way they do things at home. For example, staff in not-for-profit organizations may work in a culture of consultation before decisions are made, even if this is unusual in their home culture.

Many not-for-profits, particular those based in low-context national cultures, may be staffed by people who are from a high-context culture. For example, staff may prefer building relationships, but perhaps find it difficult to restrict their team's spending. In a different way, organizations in high-context cultures, especially those influenced by international organizations, may feel the need to follow low-context ways of working to satisfy donor requirements, even though this is not their preferred way of working. This might be in setting targets, creating work plans, and providing reports by a deadline. Most people accept these ways because their organization works efficiently as a result. Of course we need elements of both cultures for an organization to work effectively.

It is likely that whichever context we prefer and live with, we may need to use aspects of the other context in our working lives. This is particularly true of finance and finance people in what can be a low-context profession, although of course financial management is used in all cultures. When dealing with finance therefore, it is often necessary to recognize and use high-context skills to help communicate low-context information, for example, systems, deadlines, and budgets, whatever our preference. This means we have to use a wider range of context skills than just those we naturally prefer. If high- and low-context cultures are seen as being at two ends of the spectrum, then maybe we often need to be nearer the middle of the spectrum in our financial communications. If the context is too low you can appear to be rude; too high and your point may be lost.

Different professions also have ways of communicating that are appropriate when talking to others from that profession, but not necessarily when communicating with people outside. For example accountants in many countries are trained to be precise and concise in their communication. This may mean that they often provide minimal information, rather than giving long detailed answers to questions. Finance professionals may then ask for information in a way that may seem rather authoritarian or unfriendly to those who do not share their background. This can become more complex when working internationally and not everyone's training has been similar. Of course not all finance people are the same and so even with people of an equivalent professional background, communication can still be challenging. Try not to assume anything and check it out yourself.

But in some high-context national cultures, some organizations work with a low-context approach. This can be if the organization is in the capital city, is a regional office of an international organization, or has had a lot of contact with international donors.

Much of the communication about financial management can be with international donors based in low-context culture countries. And organizations receiving donor support are often in high-context countries. It is therefore essential that people in both roles respect and try to learn from each other's ways of working. Neither is better that the other; it is just the way things are. Careful listening to what each other is saying, and identifying the meaning beyond their cultural way of expressing themselves, is essential.

Partnership agreements

Not-for-profit organizations often work with partners to carry out a particular programme or activity that on their own they would not be able to deliver. Many of these arrangements involve organizations working cross-culturally. Both partners usually agree a formal written agreement in advance to identify the basis of their relationship and resolve any sensitive issues about finance.

This can be a great help to identify clearly what needs to be done by both the funding and funded partners. The agreement is a helpful addition to communication about financial and reporting issues. This is especially so when questions arise later and you can refer to the document and clarify what you originally agreed.

Financial communication between partners works well if there is one individual who acts as the contact point in each organization. It may be that these people draw on others as needed, but with one person responsible it makes it clear who will receive and forward the initial communication. Financial points to include in a partnership agreement are shown at Appendix E and more resources about cross-cultural communication are given in Written Resources and Web Resources at the end of this book.

CHAPTER 4

Practical tips for communicating internationally

We need to communicate internationally with people in different ways. We perhaps send most messages by email, but also use telephone and talk face-to-face. This chapter looks briefly at these three ways when communicating in an international context.

With all communications start by asking yourself some basic questions: why am I communicating? Who should I communicate with? When should I communicate? What do they need to know? What do I want them to know or do as a result? How will they react? How can I communicate the message most effectively? This last question will help to decide which, if any, of the following methods is most appropriate for your message or request.

Email

Communications about finance are often by email. It is a quick and easy method to use. However, it can be a very direct way of communicating and its short, impersonal style can sometimes be seen as impolite (see Box 4.1). These dos and don'ts will help to make your email effective:

Do:

- show the topic in the subject line;
- be friendly, polite, and culturally sensitive;
- make sure names are spelt correctly;
- greet people in their language, if it is different from yours;
- say why you are sending the message;
- concentrate on one main topic in each message;
- construct the message logically;
- write clearly with short paragraphs and space between them;
- check the spelling, grammar, and punctuation;

- allow the recipient to 'save face', if being critical;
- check the recipient is who you intended to send it to;
- reread the email before clicking the 'send' button.

Don't:

- use email when a personal conversation is possible and could work better;
- use technical words unless you know they will be understood;
- use abbreviations that are not well known or could be offensive;
- send attachments that might be difficult to open in different software versions – instead 'save as...' in a more widely used version;
- use capitals for words – this may be seen as shouting;
- be too personal in your greetings unless you know the person well;
- include confidential information;
- reply with a long history of emails unless absolutely necessary;
- copy all recipients to your reply, if not needed;
- click the 'send' button when you are upset – you may regret it!

Box 4.1 Communication at a distance

Last week I had this email from one of our donors:

'Not received information requested for the report. Deadline yesterday. Send immediately'.

I was so upset when I received this, I just couldn't answer it.

Also I received this email message from a different donor:

'Dear Faith, Hello, how are you? Hope you had a good weekend? Did you remember we need to finalize the donor report by tomorrow? Please send as soon as you can. Many thanks and best wishes, Tomas'.

I responded immediately.

Source: Personal communication, Zimbabwe

Email is very good when working across different time zones. Regular use is helpful to communicate practical information, but it means that we are less likely to talk to each other in person. You may prefer email but sometimes people will respond better to a more personal contact.

Telephone

Using the telephone (or computer-based telephone methods) can be a good way of communicating if you cannot meet someone face-to-face. Telephone calls (for example, with people in funding and funded partner organizations, as well as with our colleagues) can often have more impact, because they are used less frequently.

We often contact people on their work or personal cell/ mobile phones, but may find them anywhere, not just in their usual place of work, perhaps in a meeting, driving, or relaxing. Some cultures and individuals consider it impolite not to answer a call whenever it rings; others consider you rude if you answer a call when they are talking with you! Be observant and ask about appropriate behaviour in different situations, in cultures other than your own. If in doubt, switch off your phone when with other people.

When you make an international call check the time of day there. It is especially important to ask 'is this a convenient time to talk?'. If you are requesting something, you may receive a better response at some other time!

Face-to-face

If you are working with people from different countries you may only have a few opportunities to meet, even though you are regularly in contact in other ways. When these opportunities occur, it is important to use the time to build your working relationship, as well as to complete the work.

If you do not speak the same first language, you may both struggle to understand some words and meanings, as well as any regional accent, or other aspects of the culture itself. Don't give up if you struggle at first, as most people tend to adjust or tune in to what is being said after a short time. Here are some dos and don'ts about meeting face-to-face with international colleagues:

Do:

- ask about their culture in advance;
- find out the names of people you will meet, how to address them, and how to pronounce their names;
- learn a few words of greeting, if their first language is different from yours;
- listen carefully;
- speak slowly and clearly when people find it difficult to fully understand what you are saying;
- check that they have understood;
- repeat it in a different way, if something you say is not understood;
- make sure everyone has seen any paperwork before discussing the topic;
- give examples to help people understand the ideas you are trying to communicate;
- use the other person's currency in examples, rather than your own;
- talk about their financial year when giving examples of start and end dates;
- be precise and specific about what you want;
- use open-ended questions – starting with how, who, what, where, why and when, for example ask 'what questions do you have about this?', rather than 'is this all right?';
- be encouraging and value the other people and their ideas;
- take time to explain – sometimes people think they understand at the time, but realize later that they don't;
- allow others time to say what they want – ask 'what else would anyone like to add?';
- ask for and give feedback on the topics discussed. Ask 'what could we do differently?';
- summarize the discussion at the end or suggest people summarize in their own words;
- write ideas down on paper, or a board, and if possible give printed information to back up what you are saying;

- offer your business card/telephone number/email address and encourage their further thoughts, comments, or questions.

Don't:

- be offensive for example, by swearing, blaspheming (being disrespectful in using names of deities), or using culturally inappropriate behaviour;
- dress inappropriately;
- show prejudice toward age, different physical and mental abilities, education, gender, race, religion, sexual orientation, or social caste, class, or group;
- assume someone is foolish because they don't understand you;
- criticize a person in front of others, being careful to avoid this in all situations;
- talk about money, politics, or religion unless you are sensitive to other people's situation;
- use gestures, unless you are sure what they mean in the other culture.

Listen carefully to what the other person says. When working cross-culturally, remember that body language, facial expressions, and gestures may mean something different in another culture. For example, avoiding eye contact shows respect in some cultures, but in others it is considered insincere. Respecting and adapting to the new culture helps to make your communication more effective (see Box 4.2).

If you are communicating with a group face-to-face, think carefully about how you want people to sit. If you need people to participate in decision-making, make sure the seating encourages this. For example, arranging the seating in a circle or semi-circle shows that you want people to be involved in discussions, seating them in rows suggests the person at the front is the expert. Try to sit at the same level, so if you are visiting a community who are seated on the ground, sit there too.

Box 4.2 Laptop stops good communication

A visitor telephoned me to ask if he could talk to our senior staff for his research. I agreed and arranged to see him on the only day he had free in our district. It happened to be the day of our regional meeting when we were all very busy. However, I said that if we met at 9 a.m. we could see him before the meeting started at 11 a.m. We were waiting to welcome him when he arrived. He didn't talk with us, but just asked if we had internet access. We are based in a rural area, so the internet is not possible and apart from one old computer from a donor, we do not have computers. He then wanted to set up his laptop. His lead to the electricity point was not long enough but eventually we found him another one. We were all waiting for him to start, but by the time the laptop was ready it was 09.30. I could see our senior staff were becoming frustrated.

We started talking and he asked lots of questions about how we worked with our partners. He criticized us when we suggested that our work with some of our partners had not been successful. He hardly looked at us, but instead kept typing our answers into his laptop computer as we spoke. This became a barrier to our communication.

When we finished he said thank you, wished us well, and left. That was six months ago and we have not heard from him since.

Source: Personal communication, West Africa

Gender roles

The role of men and women may be different from what you are used to. In some cultures women (and sometimes men) do not shake hands. Unless you are sure, wait for others to offer you their hand. Be careful about touching people or initiating activities that are likely to involve physical contact. Use inclusive language – for example avoid using masculine words when referring to both men and women.

When socializing or planning activities, be aware of how alcohol is viewed by the culture and/or individual. Try not to make assumptions and be open and observant to what others are doing and saying. Ask people sensitively how they do things in their culture.

Resources on listening and cultural communication are provided in the Written Resources and Web Resources sections at the end of this book.

CHAPTER 5

Written financial communications

Much of our financial communication is in writing – for example emails, letters, reports, and procedures. This chapter considers how to present written communications in a way your recipient(s) can really understand.

Plain language

Clear writing is more than just avoiding technical words. It is about using a plain friendly style that is easily understood. This improves effectiveness, especially when communicating in people's second or third language. Using plain language is always helpful, but it is particularly important when working internationally (see Box 5.1).

Box 5.1 How to write clearly

- Plan what you want to say before you write;
- Organize the information into sections;
- Avoid technical words, or at least explain them;
- Use positive rather than negative phrases; write 'The cash/bank book will be much easier to control if it is updated regularly' not 'If the cash/bank book is not updated regularly, it can be more difficult to control';
- Use active not passive language; write 'We will complete the cash/bank book' rather than 'The cash/bank book will be completed';
- Turn nouns into verbs; write 'Your manager will decide if they will reimburse travel expenses' not 'All decisions about the reimbursement of travel expenses are judged by your manager';
- Remove unnecessary words: 'A new bank account is ~~in the process of~~ being set up for you';
- Be concise use no more than 15–20 words in each sentence;
- Have only one main idea for each sentence.

Source: Based on Cammack (2007)

Some finance words can be changed to make them more understandable. We sometimes use certain words out of habit, or because they are clear to us, but you can often change finance words to more understandable ones. It can be difficult to start using different words regularly, but if our aim is to communicate clearly the effort is well worthwhile. When you write think about whether it will make sense to the other person. If you are not sure, ask them for feedback and/or think again. Table 5.1 gives some alternatives to frequently used words and initials. Add your own words to this list!

Table 5.1 Using clearer words

Avoid	Use instead
According to our records	Our records show
Acknowledge (I/we acknowledge)	Thank you for
Additional	Extra
Aggregate	Total, add up
Attend	Come to
Balance brought forward	Opening balance
Balance carried forward	Closing balance
Budget virement	Budget transfer
Calculate	Work out
cf.	Compare
Chart of accounts	Budget headings
Correspond	Write
Cumulative	Added together
Deduct	Take off
Determine	Decide
Discharge	Settle, pay off
e.g.	Such as, for example
Ensure	Make sure
Establish	Create, set up
Furnish	Give, provide
i.e.	That is
Illustrate	Show, explain
Increment	Step, increase
It is known	I/we know
K	Thousand

Avoid	Use instead
LY	Last year
Marginal	Small
Not less than	At least
Not more than (five)	(Five) or less, (five) or fewer
Numerous	Many
On numerous occasions	Often
Per annum	A year
Persons	People
QTR	Quarter
Reconcile	Agree
Reduce	Cut
Remainder	The rest
Render	Send, make, give
Settle	Pay
Significant	Large
The data appears to show that	I/we think
To date	So far, up to now
Utilize	Use
Variance	Difference
Variation	Change
Verify	Check, prove
When so ever	When, whenever
With reference to	About
YTD	Year to date

Source: Some words are from the Plain English Campaign (www.plainenglish.co.uk).

People sometimes use long words because they think it makes them look intelligent or powerful. They assume that their position is more important than the work of the organization and their partners. We need to challenge this as poor communication results in the organization not being as effective as it could be. Evidence from Daniel Oppenheimer's (2006) work supports this (see Box 5.2).

Box 5.2 Plain language and intelligence

It's official. Plain English makes you seem more intelligent. According to a study from Princeton University in New Jersey, writers who use long words needlessly and choose complicated font styles are seen as less intelligent than those who stick with basic vocabulary and plain text.

The author of the study, Dr Daniel Oppenheimer, based his findings on students' responses to writing samples that had a varying difficulty of language and design. In a series of five experiments, he found that people tended to rate the intelligence of authors who wrote ... in plain language and used a clear font, as higher than those who wrote in a more complicated manner.

Dr Oppenheimer commented that 'It's important to point out that this research is not about problems with using long words but about using long words needlessly. If the best way to say something involves using a complex word, then by all means do so. But if there are several equally valid ways of expressing your ideas, you should go with the simpler one'.

Here is an example of two sentences used in the study. Readers were asked to rate the intelligence of each writer:

'The primary academic goal I have set for myself is to use my potential to the fullest'.

'The principal educational aspiration I have established for myself is to utilize my capabilities to the fullest'.

The results show that when people read something written with a more plain English approach, they actually rate the author's intelligence higher than they do those who write using large words and complicated sentences. Oppenheimer suspects people link intelligence with simpler language because we like to read things that are easy to understand.

Source: Plain English Campaign (www.plainenglish.co.uk) on Oppenheimer (2006)

How to make written communications more straightforward

A good way of making sure that all your written communication is more understandable is to review it. Using some of the points already explained in this chapter, the scales in Figure 5.1 may be useful.

Friendly and helpful style	←	Authoritarian style
Information in sections with headings	←	Written essay-style text
Understandable words	←	Technical/difficult words
Positive phrases	←	Negative phrases
Active language	←	Passive language
No unnecessary words	←	Unnecessary words
Short sentences with one main idea	←	Long sentences

Figure 5.1 Simplifying written communication

The more you move to the left of these scales, the more successful your communications are likely to be. Making instructions clear helps in many ways. The person reading them will understand more easily, but also you are more likely to receive the response you want. People will not usually ignore your request deliberately, but do so because they are not sure what you want them to do.

Boxes 5.3 and 5.4 give two examples of written communications and how they can be improved. Both examples show the original version written in a confusing style ('before') and a version that has been rewritten to make it easier to understand ('after'). Look at the letters and forms you send and see if you can write them more plainly.

Box 5.3 Making instructions easier to understand: Financial risk management systems

Before

We take the following systematic approach to risk management:
1. An analysis and identification of all possible risk exposures.
2. Evaluation of loss potential by:
   - Understanding the frequency and or/severity
   - Avoid or eliminate the risk if possible (ensuring set procedures are followed in each office e.g. segregation of duties, authorization limits, and security of assets)
   - Transferring the financial consequences to third parties or sharing it (e.g. taking out insurance, outsourcing of activities)
   - Avoiding the activity giving rise to the risk completely (e.g. a potential grant or contract not taken up)
   - Accepting the risk and absorbing it (e.g. assessed as an inherent risk that cannot be avoided if the activity is to continue).

In each office, a risk register shall be maintained containing and categorizing key risks including general enterprise-wide risk issues and country-specific operational risks in particular. Documentation of key strategies to mitigate the identified risks shall be listed in detail.

After

We approach risk management by:
1. identifying and analysing all possible risks;
2. managing risks by:
   - avoiding or eliminating the risk, if possible, by following financial procedures. For example by separating staff duties so they do not deal with the whole of any financial transaction, reducing budget authorization signing limits, and introducing tighter security of buildings and equipment;
   - sharing/giving the risk to a third party by insuring or employing an outside organization to carry out the activity;
   - avoiding the activity that creates the risk completely;
   - accepting the risk and absorbing it, for example by assessing the risk and continuing with essential work.

In each office, a *risk register* is kept. This divides risks into high, medium, or low. It includes internal and country-specific operational risks. Key strategies to deal with risks are shown in a separate document. Contact Choi (ext. 649) for more information.

Box 5.4 Making instructions easier to understand: Budget letter

Before

To begin with, the budget should be put together by adding in your own very best estimates of expenditure for the coming year. You must take into account all of the following items: the salaries (from salaries department), the cost centre's travel expenses estimate for next year (details of estimated number of kilometres and our standard rate per kilometre should be multiplied and calculated to give you the total budget figure), equipment (furnish full details of any equipment you think you need), training costs (the training department will let you have these figures based on your training needs), overheads (you will be told what the percentage to use is from the finance department's database of incremental statistics).

Any new items to include this year should be placed in the section at the bottom of the form. On numerous occasions in the past, people have put items in here without first obtaining their manager's approval. Please don't do this!

Aggregate all of these items on form X2863 from the finance department, but make sure that this year's form is used and not any from previous years, otherwise this will be rejected by the finance department. All returns shall be returned to the finance department by 10 November.

After

Please put together your budget for the period 1 January to 31 December using your best estimates. The budget form is attached.

Include

- staff salaries – Grace (ext. 384) in salaries can help you with this;
- your travel needs – your estimate of mileage for the year multiplied by the standard rate of 48 cents for each kilometre;
- equipment purchases – list each of the items;
- training – based on your needs; Sanjay (ext. 372) in the training department will help you work out the cost of courses;
- overheads – the figures are already included in the budget form.

New items

Show any new items in the section at the bottom of the budget form. Make sure your manager approves these first.

Next steps

Add up the amounts and enter in the 'total' box at the end of the form. Please return it to finance as soon as you can but by *10 November*. If you need any help in filling in the form telephone Mustafa (ext. 309).

Writing financial procedures

Organizations will often communicate information about their finance systems by producing financial procedures. These instructions are used by finance staff and sometimes also aimed at non-finance staff. They are an excellent way to help establish good financial controls. If working internationally it is common to send copies of the procedures to other countries where the language they are written in may not be the staff's first language.

Typically financial procedures will include: how to operate cash and bank accounts; which post holder can sign cheques; expenditure and income controls; who authorizes payments; how expenses are claimed; how income is paid in; and the budgeting process – what is required to plan budgets, how are they monitored, and who is responsible.

Most financial procedures are written by finance staff who can use technical words that non-finance people may not understand. Always think about the person using the financial procedures when you write them. Will the readers understand the language or do you need to translate the document? How will different words and ideas work when they are translated? Ask how much information is needed. Keep the content as short as possible but remember to say where more information can be found.

Here is a summary of good practice for writing procedures:

- Identify who are the readers and what experience of finance they actually have.
- Follow the suggestions on how to write clearly on page 47;
- Make the document as short and clear as possible;
- Split the information into sections, with separate headings. Consider numbering each paragraph;
- Follow a logical pattern in the content. For example start with budgeting, if that is the first financial task the reader is likely to do;
- Don't fill the page with information – leave plenty of empty space;
- Make it look attractive and interesting. In longer documents use different coloured paper for different sections;

include boxes, diagrams, bulleted lists, and pictures to break up the text; use different fonts;

- Ask someone else (for example a non-finance colleague) to read through the document and give feedback;
- Decide who needs a copy of the full document. If financial procedures are just sent to managers, they may stay on their shelf and never be used. If the full document is sent to those who only need one paragraph, they may never find the part they need;
- Use other ways of communicating your message – especially for those who do not read, or prefer oral ways of communicating, or if the document is not written in an individual's first language. Perhaps highlight parts of the document in regular meetings, hold a special training event, or maybe produce a computer presentation of the highlights. Use key parts in induction and other training;
- Include a list of financial words with clear definitions. People may use this simply to find out what a particular word really means;
- Update the procedures regularly;
- Translate materials where possible into the reader's first language.

CHAPTER 6

Using numbers

Now that we have looked at written communications, this chapter focuses on the presentation of numerical information. It challenges us to review what we currently send or receive, and to make it more accessible. It includes good practice for adding notes to financial reports and suggests other techniques for encouraging people to use the information.

Most financial communications include numerical data that can be confusing. Many people who receive it may say that they do not really understand the information. Others may be too embarrassed to say anything, but some will understand it fully. Information needs to be presented in a way that is easily understandable by everyone, including a non-finance person.

The finance people who present the information can be speaking their own 'finance language' and yet they expect non-finance people to understand it. Some non-finance people will use this 'language' too, and become very good at it. However, sometimes the 'language' can be spoken very badly, so even other finance people who speak it themselves find it impossible to understand.

How do your documents look?

So how can it be done better? The starting point is simply to talk with and listen to the people receiving the document. Find out what they understand, what they find difficult, and what they really need. Then work with them to improve the presentation and the content. Firstly present it so that there are no words or abbreviations that are not understandable to a non-technical person.

The following example (Table 6.1) compares budgeted figures with actual income and expenditure. This is based on a real example. The comments written around the report explain some of the changes needed to make it more understandable to a non-finance person. A similar approach in identifying what could be improved could be taken with any numerical information.

Table 6.2 show a revised and clearer version of the same information.

Use of explanatory notes

A budget and actual report may be used by a range of people who do not know the detail of the organization or activity, for example senior and other managers, members of the management committee, partners, donors and fundraisers. It is good practice to add notes that explain the reason for any differences between the budget and actual income and expenditure. Donors will often see this as a professional way of reflecting on what is happening, which adds credibility to your programme management.

Notes are sometimes shown as a numbered list at the bottom of the table (often with an extra column on the right hand side with a reference number to the notes), or if space, there is an extra column at the right hand side of the table for the note itself.

The notes can be short. For example, if the travel expenditure was less than the budgeted amount, a note could state 'limited travel (only) in the last three months due to heavy rains'. This may also help the person writing the report to remember the reason later in the year. Notes should state whether the figures included have or have not been 'adjusted'. For example, electricity might include not only the amount paid, but also an amount that is due to be paid by the date of the report (although it will not actually be paid until after the date of the report). This is known as items paid in arrears, or an 'accruals adjustment' (see Appendix B). This kind of adjustment makes it possible to compare the 'budget' and 'actual' figures for the same period of time. If the figures haven't been adjusted in this way it is useful to state that too.

Ideally the main task of monitoring the budget and the activity it represents is done by someone who is physically close

Table 6.1 Example of budget and actual report before revision, with comments and possible changes

Handwritten annotations: Title needed · Both columns needed? · QTR, YTD, LY not clear – show in full · Confusing – put date in title · Column not needed · 2nd annual · What do these mean · Move to right · Delete · Bold → · Sub-total needed · in full · Delete all figures after decimal point

PERIOD: 311211

	Original budget	Working budget	QTR budget	QTR actual	YTD budget	YTD actual	YTD variance	%YTD buget	LY actual	FC DEC
	8686	8687	27787	7877	7877	7789	7877	98898	8988	0
Overall summary										
Income										
Grants	777877.49	777877.49	194469.37	168000.00	583408.12	560376.32	-23031.80	-3.95	700021	0
Donations	179496.39	179496.39	44874.10	38239.38	134622.29	117378.04	-17244.25	-12.81	150381	0
Other	288379.68	288379.68	72094.93	62293.48	216284.78	192374.31	-23910.47	-11.06	235495	0
Mld-dons	14165.99	14165.99	3541.50	5382.82	10624.49	12313.94	1689.45	15.90	14953	0
Total	1259919.55	1259919.55	314979.90	273915.68	944939.68	882442.61	-62497.07	-6.61	1100850	0
Expenditure										
Staff costs	467726.32	467726.32	116931.58	114392.10	350794.74	340219.19	10575.55	3.01	479301	0
Temporary	56403.29	56403.29	14100.82	12298.09	42302.47	32198.03	10104.44	23.89	43829	0
Volunteers	494.10	494.10	123.53	160.37	370.58	394.65	-24.07	-6.50	486	0
Staff trn'g	38829.20	38829.20	9707.30	6398.91	29121.90	21482.46	7639.44	26.23	37287	0
Travel	99633.71	99633.71	24908.43	23948.59	74725.28	78346.29	-3621.01	-4.85	110392	0
Advy/pubs	387473.30	387473.30	96868.33	194834.48	290604.98	273127.84	17477.14	6.01	343212	0
Office	29614.37	29614.37	7403.59	7928.17	22210.78	21387.40	823.38	3.71	28349	0
Postage/tel	57683.29	57683.29	14420.82	12487.29	43262.47	39471.48	3790.99	8.76	55282	0
Repairs	5763.00	5763.00	1440.75	300.21	4322.25	2347.16	1975.09	45.70	8239	0
Prems	95822.75	95822.75	23955.69	39418.54	71867.06	79384.28	-7517.22	-10.46	89347	0
Miscell's	19909.22	19909.22	4977.31	3218.47	14931.92	12384.10	2547.82	17.06	16239	0
Other	567.00	567.00	141.75	200.00	425.25	566.39	-141.14	-33.19	452	0
Sub	596832.93	596832.93	149208.24	258387.16	447624.71	428668.65	18956.06	4.23	541120	0
Total	1259919.55	1259919.55	314979.90	415585.22	944939.68	901309.27	43630.41	4.62	1212415	0
Surpl/Def	0.00	0.00	0.00	-141669.54	0.00	-18866.66	-18866.66	#DIV/0!	2313265	0

Table 6.2 Example of budget and actual report, after revision and rounding

EASTERN PROVINCE COMMUNITY CENTRE

Budget and actual report for period from 1 April 20.. To 31 December 20..

	Annual budget 1 Apr 20.. to 31 Mar 20..	Budget 1 Oct to 31 Dec 20..	Actual 1 Oct to 31 Dec 20..	Budget 1 Apr to 31 Dec 20..	Actual 1 Apr to 31 Dec 20..	Difference 1 Apr to 31 Dec 20..	% difference 1 Apr to 31 Dec 20..	Comparison Actual last year 1 Apr to 31 Dec 20..
	€	€	€	€	€	€	%	€
Income								
Grants	777,877	194,469	168,000	583,408	560,376	-23,032	-4	500,021
Donations	179,496	44,874	38,239	134,622	117,378	-17,244	-13	100,381
Sales of publications	288,380	72,095	62,293	216,285	192,374	-23,911	-11	195,495
Membership fees	14,166	3,542	5,383	10,625	12,314	1,689	16	11,953
Total: all income	**1,259,919**	**314,980**	**273,915**	**944,940**	**882,442**	**-62,498**	**-7**	**807,850**
Expenditure								
Staff salaries	467,726	116,932	114,392	350,795	340,219	10,576	3	379,301
Temporary staff	56,403	14,101	12,298	42,302	32,198	10,104	24	33,829
Volunteers expenses	494	124	160	371	395	-24	-6	486
Staff training	38,829	9,707	6,399	29,122	21,482	7,640	26	27,287
Travel	99,634	24,908	23,949	74,725	78,346	-3,621	-5	80,392
Total: staff and travel	*663,086*	*165,772*	*157,198*	*497,315*	*472,640*	*24,675*	*5*	*521,295*
Advocacy/publications	387,473	96,868	194,835	290,605	273,128	17,477	6	243,212
Office running costs	29,615	7,403	7,928	22,211	21,387	824	4	21,349
Postage/telephone	57,683	14,421	12,487	43,263	39,472	3,791	9	45,282
Repairs of building	5,763	1,441	300	4,322	2,347	1,975	46	8,239
Premises costs	95,823	23,956	39,419	71,867	79,384	-7,517	-10	59,347
Miscellaneous	19,909	4,977	3,218	14,932	12,384	2,548	17	16,239
Bank charges	567	142	200	425	567	-142	-33	452
Total: office costs	*596,833*	*149,208*	*258,387*	*447,625*	*428,669*	*18,956*	*4*	*394,120*
Total: all expenditure	**1,259,919**	**314,980**	**415,585**	**944,940**	**901,309**	**43,631**	**5**	**915,415**
Income less expenditure	**0**	**0**	**-141,670**	**0**	**-18,867**	**-18,867**		**-107,565**

A minus sign (-) shows more budget than actual for income items, and more actual than budget for expenditure.

Adjustments have been made for items paid in advance and in arrears.

to what is happening (although they do not usually prepare the financial information as well, except in small organizations). This is the person who can make best use of the information and respond to it quickly. However other people, for example donors, managers, and partners may also need to see the information. For these people the notes are an excellent way of knowing what is happening, and often save a lot of questions from donors and others later on!

Writing notes can have a very positive effect on the activity. Reflecting on what has happened helps the person managing the activity to feed this knowledge back into the programme. It is also possible to identify any errors in the figures. For these reasons, it is preferable that the budget manager rather than a finance person should write these notes.

Good practice in presenting numbers

Do:

- ask users how they want the information presented;
- make the amount of information provided suitable for the audience: detailed for managers, summarized for others (with an option for more detail if required);
- add notes to clarify large differences in the budget and actual figures;
- use no more than one side of paper, if possible;
- include a title, show dates covered by table as a whole, and for each column;
- show dates of the period, for example 1 Oct 20.. to 31 Dec 20.., rather than 3 months to 31 Dec 20.. It can be useful to also quote the period covered, such as '3 months';
- write the date as '31 Dec 20..' or 'Dec 31, 20..' rather than '3112..' or '1231..';
- show budget codes only if those receiving the information know them well;
- use full words rather than abbreviations wherever possible;
- put title, column titles, heading such as income and expenditure, and total figures in bold to make them more obvious;

- check addition;
- show clearly which figures (sub-totals) add together to give the total figure;
- use commas to make figures clearer, if possible;
- state the currency the report is in unless obvious;
- state whether adjustments have been made for amounts in arrears and in advance;
- explain what positive and negative figures mean.

Don't:

- show any non-essential information;
- include amounts after the decimal point – round to the nearest whole number;
- use accountants' abbreviations (for example 'ytd' for year to date, 'qtr' for quarter, 'ly' for last year);
- use commas between numbers if they mean something different in countries that receive the information.

Asking questions about numerical financial reports

Try to answer any possible questions in the explanatory notes, but managers, donors, partners, and others often find there are still outstanding points.

When asking questions about financial information, be aware of the cultural issues raised in Chapters 2 and 3. Finance in many cultures is a sensitive issue and needs to be handled with care, especially if using email or letters. Remember not to be too critical but instead balance positive and negative comments. If you or a colleague have a chance to visit the person it is often easier to address sensitive issues face-to-face rather than in writing. Telephone conversations are another option if you think that would help to find the information you need.

Remember to:

- be sensitive;
- be friendly in your approach;
- put the positive feedback/questions first and last, and any negatives in the middle;
- ask for help rather than be critical;

- whatever you need to ask, try to maintain a good relationship with the individual.

'Budgeting buddy'

If you receive numerical financial information (annual financial statements, budget and actual reports, cost information) and you are responsible for authorizing or monitoring them, it may take some time before you manage to review the document. You may like to use short, regular meetings between a finance and non-finance person to discuss the information (see Chapter 2).

Another approach for non-finance people is to find someone (a 'budgeting buddy') who also has documents to review, and arrange a time to meet with them to look through both sets. By doing this together you can review everything more quickly, and more importantly you might discover important points that you would have missed. You then have a list of questions to follow up, and you don't have to worry that the document is still in your in-tray!

Signing off

A technique often used to show that financial information has been approved is called 'signing off'. This is usually done by a manager, and involves someone signing a document to say they are satisfied with the content. Sometimes this will be an approval to spend money, or recognizing that a piece of financial work (such as agreeing your records with the bank account records) has been completed. This is an important way of taking care of the money within organizations, and it is often performed by non-finance managers.

Sometimes managers sign without really understanding what the document means and the consequences. If this is the case, it is important that someone explains what is expected and exactly what is being approved. It is the responsibility of senior managers to make sure this happens. It is important that managers who are given this task of signing know enough to challenge other staff about their expenditure if necessary, before signing.

The challenge

The challenge to everyone who produces numerical financial information is to make it understandable. Keep testing it out with people who receive the information and find it difficult. Ask them what they do and do not understand. Spend time with them. Use this feedback as valuable information to continue to improve the quality of the documents you circulate, and as a result to improve the quality of your financial communication.

CHAPTER 7

Communicating financial management with stakeholders

The aim of this chapter is to consider the various groups who use an organization's financial communication, both internally and externally. Communication to these groups and individuals is sometimes from finance people, but a range of non-finance people also need to present and receive financial information. Good practice is given for each group of recipients.

Management committee/governing body/trustees

The management committee has a number of responsibilities for financial management, including (Cammack, 1997):

- setting objectives;
- approving and regularly monitoring the budget;
- approving the annual financial statements;
- appointing the auditors;
- receiving and acting on the audit report and recommendations;
- making sure there is adequate money and funding;
- appointing adequate finance staff;
- making sure there is a high standard of financial management;
- reporting to donors on what has been received;
- complying with national legislation and regulations.

Some of these tasks are legal requirements, and all the members of the management committee can be personally liable if things go wrong. It is therefore important that the committee members understand the information given to them and they have a member who is specifically responsible for communicating financial management and giving it a high profile (see Box 7.1).

Box 7.1 Can we do without a finance person?

An organization considered that its programme activities were the only reason for existing. It has always struggled to receive enough funding, and over many years its staff and premises have been reduced. Their finance department has not been seen as important and as a result the quality of the information produced has become less and less useful.

One casualty of the cuts was the finance department itself. Not only was the number of staff reduced by half, five years ago, but also none of the staff other than the head of finance now has any formal qualification.

The head of finance reports to an operations manager, a human resource (HR) professional, who in turn reports to the director of services but she has no qualification in either HR or finance. The director represents both HR and finance departments at the staff board meeting each week. However the chief executive does not understand finance either, so always delegates financial issues to the director of services.

Until about three years ago, the staff board meeting discussed finance with a report comparing actual income and expenditure to the budget. However the staff board realized that no one really understood the report and because the finance department struggled to produce it in time, they decided that it was no longer needed. The board still approves the budget each year, but that is their only involvement with financial management.

Their voluntary management committee meets every three months and only discusses finance to decide what activities they might stop doing. There is no professional financial input – the treasurer of the management committee took on the job because there was no one else but doesn't understand his role; none of the members can remember the last time the head of finance came to their meeting.

Recently a new member came to their first management committee meeting. He had already talked with the head of finance and realized that the organization has only enough money to keep going for another five months. He was shocked that there was so little financial information available at the meeting. He suggested that one reason the organization is declining is that finance is ignored and decision-making is badly informed. He proposed a qualified accountant be appointed to a new senior post of finance director, who would be a member of the staff board, manage the finance department, and attend and brief the management committee. Some members argued this would be too expensive.

Source: From a UK training course

This voluntary role is sometimes called a treasurer. In smaller organizations it is not always possible to find someone who has a financial background. If so, it is important to seek professional advice from staff or external accountants, although legally these people often cannot be members of the management committee. In large organizations the treasurer is ideally an experienced qualified accountant.

The role of treasurer is important for building bridges around financial management within organizations. Organizations whose management committees do not have such a role are less likely to be sustainable because strong financial advice and information are crucial at this level for an organization to continue to achieve its aims.

Much of what has already been said in Chapters 4 and 5 about presenting written and numerical information applies to the documents given to the management committee. Make sure the information needed for the meeting is circulated in advance so members have a chance to read it and ask informed questions at the meeting. Most members may not understand finance in detail so it must be communicated well both in the documents and in any presentations to meetings, following good practice for financial communications, such as that in Cammack (2007):

Do:

- be clear and concise;
- focus on the key points;
- use simple language;
- explain any technical words;
- see the issue from the other person's point of view;
- show the information visually;
- keep people interested: ask your listeners 'is this making sense?';
- highlight any lighter parts – laughter helps communication;
- give plenty of opportunity for questions;
- encourage people to ask for more information;
- work with users to improve the clarity of financial information and systems;
- provide training where needed.

Don't:

- use technical words before explaining what they mean;
- talk for too long – a few minutes is often enough;
- confuse people with financial concepts and jargon.

Analysis of the financial information

The management committee has an important role in questioning and controlling the organization's income and expenditure. At least some of the members need to fully understand what is presented to them and ask questions. If members feel unable to do this there is probably a need for some financial training. Certainly a new treasurer and new members need induction and training so they can be effective in this aspect of their role.

Sometimes larger organizations also have a finance sub-committee of two or three members of the management committee and staff. Its role is to look in more detail at financial information and systems. Even where such a sub-committee exists it is still important that the management committee receives full financial reports, approves the budget, appoints the auditors, and receives the report and recommendations from the auditors.

Members

Some, but not all, organizations have a membership in addition to the management committee. Some members may be individuals, others may be organizational members. They may be responsible for electing the management committee, and, if there is no management committee, financially responsible for the organization. In other organizations it is a looser form of membership that could be seen more as 'supporters', with little or no general or financial responsibility.

Whichever model of membership is followed, it is good practice to keep members regularly up to date with reports about the financial situation of the organization. This is often done through newsletters and annual reports. The information needs to be presented simply, perhaps showing percentages through bar and pie charts with just some of the key items and totals shown in figures. Further information and the full accounts should always be offered for anyone who wants more details.

Staff board and senior managers

If there is a staff board, for example the departmental managers in larger organizations, it is important that its members receive clear financial advice from someone who understands the information well and can communicate it in an understandable way. All the comments about communicating information clearly to the management committee also apply to the staff board.

This finance person needs to hold an equal status to other board members, so that decisions can be jointly made. If the finance role is seen as being of a lower status, it is likely that the finance person may be overruled in decisions. Finance and the information it provides may not be taken seriously throughout the entire organization, with negative consequences.

All staff (finance and non-finance)

Earlier chapters cover financial communication between finance and non-finance staff. However some financial messages need to be communicated to all staff by management. The funding of many not-for-profit organizations can be uncertain and if economic times are difficult it is vital for all staff to know how secure their job and salary are. This is as much about good staff relations as about finance, but it is important to keep everyone regularly informed.

Make sure ways of communicating are appropriate. Don't confuse people with too many figures and use visual presentations as much as possible. Follow the good practice list of dos and don'ts for financial communications presented earlier in this chapter.

Staff often need to learn a range of financial and other skills, particularly programme staff who deal directly with partner organizations and community groups. Learning from colleagues who have these skills can build strong relationships, and make your communication more effective outside your organization.

It is important too that all staff have opportunities to keep learning about financial issues. Consider how often staff in your organization (especially administrative staff) have opportunities to take part in training activities. Also make sure that those without formal qualifications, those who work verbally rather than through reading or writing, and poor and marginalized partner and community groups, are included in developing their skills (see Box 7.2).

Partners, community groups, and service users

International, national, and local not-for-profits communicate approved budgets and often copies of their annual financial statements to their groups. However, they sometimes find it challenging to communicate this and other information in an appropriate way.

It is important for partners, community groups, and service users to be informed how money given by a donor, for their ultimate benefit, has been used. For example, information on what is deducted from the original amount before it reaches the community. This could relate to a specific activity with which users will be familiar, and a summary of costs related to the provision of that activity. Ideally this would be in visual format. Be sensitive about any salary information that can be linked to an individual. Make sure those reading the information have a way of providing feedback. For example who they should contact with questions. This will help to increase the participation of the users in their activities, which in turn may strengthen and sustain the impact of their/your programme.

Keep it simple, for example:

- use paper or a whiteboard to present the key areas of your budget with objectives;
- use visual presentations. Include a bar or pie chart in a newsletter to show where the money has come from and

Box 7.2 'Polyvalence': An interaction of people's skills

We noticed that our staff were excellent in their own work, but when it comes to other areas of work needed within organizations, they didn't have the same level of expertise. This made it difficult when they were expected to use a range of skills with our partner groups, and also for us to understand the work that each of us did. We decided to encourage our staff to participate in all the different work activities of our own organization. We started by making sure that they all knew what we were doing in the implementation and evaluation of our programme of activities. This included programme, administration, and finance staff. Everyone was involved in learning what each other did. We called the process 'Polyvalence', which we think of as meaning interacting with many skills together.

As an example I was the sponsorship manager and started to learn about programme financial control even though I did not have a financial background. Of course, it was not the same as a professional audit of the programme, but I was then able to give the finance manager all the relevant information from our offices and he could identify if, and when, further investigations were needed.

This is all the more important for the financial staff. We noticed that financial staff are generally only concerned by their figures and sometimes, they even think their work is the most important because it is linked to managing money. Thanks to this new concept of Polyvalence, financial staff clearly notice that the other positions of the organization have the same importance. They realize that if something is not working correctly in a part of the organization, it can seriously affect the finance level and the whole organization.

All this has meant that also I and my colleagues were able to help our partners even more. Each of us could undertake, monitor, and evaluate several areas of work.

Polyvalence requires each member of staff to be committed, and there needs to be a high level of team spirit. However we all gain from the process, we have learned a wider range of skills that we can use within our organization and in helping our partners, and we feel better skilled and motivated. We understand more clearly the work that our colleagues are doing. Overall, Polyvalence is a training process for staff with great results for organizations and partners.

Source: Christian Children's Fund of Canada, Burkina Faso

where it has gone to. Computer spreadsheet programs can easily convert figures into charts;

- draw a poster with similar details that can be displayed where communities and service users gather;
- think about publishing information in local newspapers or on radio;
- give out printed copies of financial information, summarized on no more than one page, following the good practice in communicating financial information listed above;
- call a meeting to discuss financial priorities, plans, and reports, explaining what they mean for their community; invite a skilled communicator who understands finance;
- use meetings to present audit findings;
- provide opportunities for feedback and questions;
- translate materials into the language(s) used.

If working with partners who themselves work with community groups and service users, it is good to ask questions such as 'what financial information do you give to people you work with?', 'what feedback do you receive about this information?', and 'could you do anything differently to keep the groups better informed?'.

Find appropriate ways of telling your partners about your financial position, your plans for allocating money to them, and any limitations you have. Keep them informed if fundraising is not so good, and about policy changes that may affect them. Tell them too how you use your own funds. This will help them to decide their own priorities and make their own decisions.

Monitor how the communication works and use feedback to improve next time. Make sure that poorer and vulnerable members of the community are not left out of these discussions. If you are working in a community where gender issues are sensitive, you may, for example, need to find ways of reaching the female members of the community by perhaps using a female facilitator.

Building the financial management capacity of small partners is an important starting point for improving their communication and programme effectiveness. Whether or not your organization currently supports capacity-building, it is worth asking partners 'how can we help you build your financial management capacity?' and 'do you have other donors who help build your financial management capacity?'.

Donors

Institutional donors

Many not-for-profit organizations rely on institutional donors (that is organizations rather than individuals) for funding and to continue their work. Strong communication between not-for-profits and donors is important to:

- make sure that funding will continue in the way you want;
- access other kinds of support (for example, capacity-building);
- recognize how you are being asked to report;
- maintain credibility of your organization's financial management and programme activities.

Much of the relationship involves financial information – from budgets that are needed in proposals, to financial reports when the money is spent. How the relationship is managed can vary from one organization to another. In some it will all be through one programme person who communicates about everything; in others it may be through a fundraiser who uses programme and finance colleagues to provide them with the relevant information.

All organizations occasionally need to look at how their communications with donors can work to the best advantage for themselves and their partners. Ask questions such as:

- Who are our best people to receive donor representatives when they visit?
- Who are our best communicators?
- How can we best put across our strengths?
- How well can our main contact person talk about programme, funding, and finance?
- Do our fundraisers know enough about our programme to convince donors to fund?

- Do our fundraisers know enough about our finances to convince donors to fund?
- Have finance and fundraising staff visited our donors?
- Can our programme staff talk about finance convincingly with donors?
- Should our finance staff be the main contact for donor finance staff?

These questions need to the looked at to make sure your organization makes the most of its relationship with donors. Sometimes when finance people visit the donor finance staff, they provide solutions to some of the practical aspects of reporting and accounting issues. They can also give the donor reassurance that the organization takes the financial issues seriously. The cost of such visits can sometimes be paid back many times over through improved relationships, time and cost savings, and additional funding. See partnership agreements in Appendix E and Box 7.3.

Individual donors

Individual donors are likely to include a wide range of people, so when communicating financial management information it is important not to make assumptions. Information needs to be clear and ideally in a visual form (for example pie charts and diagrams). Financial communications should always include a clear statement that the accounts have been audited (but only if they have) and details of where users can obtain more information or copies of the full accounts. The financial information should complement other information about the activities, show that the money has been well spent, and that it has made a difference.

Fundraisers

The relationship between a fundraiser(s) and a member(s) of the finance staff can be crucial to the organization's survival. Where the relationship works well, funding is more

---

Box 7.3 Keeping good relationships with donors

At Medair, we have found it crucial to build strong long-term relationships with our institutional donors. Whenever possible a member of the finance team visits them, sometimes in their own country. Although this can be expensive, the relationships it creates can lead to additional funding that repays the investment many times over. This strong relationship based on our proven commitment to accountability and transparency has, for example, helped us to negotiate and increase the percentage that we receive toward our core costs.

When reporting back to donors we make sure that the reports are a joint effort between the programme and finance teams. Of course both need to know something about each other's work, but fewer misunderstandings happen this way. We often find it helpful to let our finance team talk with the donor's finance people, and our programme team with their programme people.

Institutional donors sometimes hold annual partnership meetings to review grant and project results, discuss future strategy, changes in direction, and to consider risks. Having finance staff attend these meetings, especially line managers and some from the field accounting and reporting teams, has proved extremely beneficial.

We try to respond positively to any of their audit issues, and this commitment to changing processes and procedures when necessary has helped strengthen donor relationships. Such responsiveness helps maintain or secure a 'preferred partner relationship' with the donor. This is crucial to sustain future programme delivery.

Source: Medair, Switzerland

---

likely to be forthcoming and the programme activities able to flourish.

Both fundraisers and finance staff need support from each other for their work to be successful. Fundraisers are likely to need help from finance staff to:

- understand what is required by long-term objectives/strategic financial plans (if prepared);
- go through the annual budget well before the start of the year;
- explain technical aspects of accounting patiently, for example, depreciation, reserves (see Appendix B), and the

annual financial statements, and particularly how these can be best presented to donors;

- be flexible in presenting information in different ways to donors;
- provide costings for each unit (for example cost per child vaccinated);
- discuss how overheads can be justified and explained in funding applications;
- agree any differences between income recorded in the finance and fundraising records;
- work together to prepare for joint meetings, both within the organization and with donors;
- review applications from a financial viewpoint before submission;
- be a critical friend.

Finance staff need support from fundraisers to:

- give their best estimate of the income budget and when funds will arrive;
- clarify reporting requirements on income restricted for a certain purpose;
- explain proposed budgets and any subsequent changes;
- agree fundraising income with that shown in the accounting records;
- send acknowledgements to, and keep good relationships with, donors;
- include precise dates and references on all appeals and funding applications, so funds received can easily be allocated to the right place.

Finance staff

Whether you are a finance or non-finance person, communicating about finance is often done by someone who knows or is thought to know about finance. In many not-for-profits and especially small organizations this role may be played by an administrator or a finance officer. In large organizations there may be several people or an entire department who deal with finance. It is always important that finance is understood in its wider organizational context. Ideally the finance person or some of the finance team will have experience from other organizations.

Smaller organizations often use a mixture of skills to improve financial communication. The one finance person may concentrate on the day-to-day work and production of information. The manager/director may take responsibility for the organizational aspect and communication with the management committee, and professional accounting expertise may then be drawn on as needed from an individual or outside firm of accountants. Larger organizations may have their own paid staff doing all these roles.

When communicating with a finance person/department it is useful to understand some differences between staff roles to make sure you are contacting the right person. In all but small organizations it is useful to have a list of names of the finance staff, their contact details, the areas they can answer questions about, and if possible photographs too.

Not all finance staff will understand all the technical accounting words, or exactly what the systems do. It can be helpful for non-finance people to find someone they can talk with who understands the finance system, but whose understanding is only a small step ahead of theirs. All organizations need someone who understands finance fully and can communicate in non-technical words to others who need to know. Where this does not happen, it needs to be addressed through training and/or a review of the staffing.

Finance staff need to respond to any requests for information with an encouraging and positive attitude. More details about developing these approaches are shown in Chapter 2.

Suppliers

It is important to build strong long-term relationships between finance and their key suppliers such as banks, auditors, and software providers. Organizations need to keep good relationships with all their suppliers and in larger organizations this may be done by a separate purchasing department. The relationship should aim to help suppliers find out more about the kind of work your organization is doing, so they may also feel a sense of commitment. Good relationships can help to strengthen the work you do, and may sometimes lead to grants, donations, or 'in-kind' support.

CHAPTER 8

Facilitating training and learning to communicate finance

This chapter looks at communicating financial management through training and learning. It looks at practical issues of how training can be designed and delivered to build strong relationships between different stakeholders.

Building relationships through training and learning

One of the barriers to good financial communication is that those involved may not be skilled enough to explain things clearly, or not have enough knowledge about finance and financial management to understand what is needed. The impact of these barriers can be reduced through training and learning courses.

Sometimes finance staff deliver financial courses for their non-finance colleagues. These events can offer important stages in organizational and personal growth. The courses need to be well facilitated with an interactive approach. An external facilitator may help to achieve this, but it is always useful to have some of the finance staff present to answer organizational questions and also to build relationships with course members. The external facilitator should aim to encourage this relationship building by recognizing the times when finance staff themselves are best placed to lead a session.

Providing well-facilitated shared courses can also help both groups to overcome some of the negative perceptions identified and listed on page 8 in Chapter 2. It can be an opportunity to share common knowledge and concerns, and see how both groups could cooperate more effectively together for the benefit of the organization. Not only can training and learning improve the financial management skills and communication of individuals, but they can then also influence partner organizations and the programme activities in which they are involved.

Identifying the need for training

The first stage of training and learning is to identify the needs of those to be trained. Training needs analysis (TNA) makes sure that training is the best approach, and that it is targeted with the right material for the right people and at the right time. TNA's aim is to identify the difference or gap between what happens at present and what is required for an individual or group to perform at their expected level. A useful question to ask is 'what do you want to be able to do differently at the end of the training?'. It is also important that the organization and individuals see any previous mistakes as an opportunity to learn. Any analysis should be handled sensitively and therefore be, and seen to be, a positive experience for those involved.

Kerry Thomas and Theresa Mellon (1995) identify the following points where there can be training and learning needs:

- *changes are forecast or happening*, for example, when someone is appointed to a new job as a manager and lacks budgeting skills;
- *problems are being experienced*, for example, a decision-making committee has to reduce expenditure, and the person providing the information does not have the skills to explain how much money is available;
- *potential is not being fully utilized*, for example, a member of the finance team is working with partners when they visit the office and explaining how to put together basic records. This person has the potential to deliver training courses.

TNA helps to identify what is required for individuals to develop. It helps to target limited training resources where they will be most effective. General morale and job satisfaction can be improved if individuals know that TNA is taken seriously. Analysing training needs takes time and requires managers and staff to be committed to the process. However, undertaking training and learning without some form of needs analysis can be ineffective and expensive. There are a number of ways in which the information can be gathered. Organizations often start the process through their management systems (for example, through annual staff reviews). Techniques for capturing the information about needs can include: observing what happens, talking with people about their expectations and challenges, and asking people to complete a questionnaire.

Training is not always the answer. Sometimes there are organizational or personnel problems that need to be addressed in other ways. For example, by making more resources available, identifying changes needed to provide more tools for the job (which may also result in a training need), providing more support by a manager, giving 'permission' to someone to use their skills more fully, making staff and other roles clear, and sharing someone's expertise more widely.

Approaches to financial management training and learning

Interactive (or participatory) training approaches – that is, allowing the learner to be actively involved in the process, rather than just listening to someone talking – are essential for training in financial subjects. It means that people learn by doing. Whether the training is with one person, a small group, or in a workshop, provide hands-on training for the new task to be learned. It is important that learners can listen and talk about finance topics, but the true test of whether learning has been effective is whether the task can be completed successfully. Relate the training to the learners' everyday work and give them practical tools that they can use immediately.

To improve communication with non-literate groups and those who struggle with the language used, include diagrams and visual activities. These are good for all learners and provide variation from the spoken and written word. Write key words and ideas on paper or a board, so that the topics can be understood more easily. Be willing to go over the material again, and include regular reviews of what has been covered. Find fun ways for learners to remember what they have learned.

Different learning styles

Different people learn in different ways and it is important to recognize this when activities are designed. When organizing courses, have various options that will meet everyone's learning styles. In many cultures it is more natural to learn face-to-face rather than through the written word.

Different ways of learning include: on-the-job training, face-to-face instructions and discussions, teaching someone else, working with partner organizations, programme visits, participating in an external course, short training sessions as part of regular meetings, interactive computer packages, networking with others doing similar work, personal study though reading books and other resources, and internal courses.

Ask people about their preferred way of learning and try to design the training based on this. With individuals and small groups it is perhaps easier to match the training to the learners' needs.

Designing training and learning

All the training needs can often not be met in the time available. It is important then for a training facilitator to plan the material needed, by putting together what the learners say they need, identifying the key objectives for the organization(s), and their own knowledge of what is helpful.

The technique for deciding what goes in is often described as: 'must learn, should learn, and could learn'. Concentrate first on the 'must learn'. It is usually better to cover only a limited amount of material fully, rather than to cover all the material more briefly. Don't expect people to need or want to know everything you know. Keep prioritizing the material and concentrate on a few key points that they will remember and use.

Figure 8.1 What to include and what not to include in a training session

Make sure that the content is targeted to the learner's or group of learners' needs. Write learning objectives. These are sentences that describe the purpose of each of the training topics. They need to describe what the learner will be able to *do*, rather than what they will *know* or *understand* by the end of the course. The following example shows the style where 'explain', 'monitor', and 'create' are all 'doing' words.

At the end of this session, the learner should be able to:

- explain the main aspects of budget management;
- monitor a budget and actual report;
- create tools to improve budgeting monitoring.

If you are inviting people to a training event, these objectives will show what topics are included and hopefully make sure that the right people attend the right event. They also help training facilitators and learners focus on what is being covered during the course. They make it possible to measure how effective the event has been.

A full description of writing learning objectives is outside the scope of this book, but helpful materials are listed in the Written Resources and Web Resources sections at the end of the book.

Training and learning delivery

Most financial management training courses will be with adults. Adults come with previous work and life experience, and this may be relevant to what is being learned.

People may be worried about the idea of learning something new, and may feel especially anxious about financial training.

It may remind them of mathematics lessons at school, or they may fear looking foolish among people they know. Facilitators have to work hard to reassure learners and if necessary, talk with individuals and groups about their concerns. Always try to be positive and not critical. Always start off with the basics and use a step-by-step and interactive approach where learners are actively involved in doing rather than just listening.

At the start of the course address people's worries by using some fun introductory activities to help them to relax. Books with examples of suitable activities are shown in the Written Resources section. Ask learners what their expectations are (even if this information has been already gathered) and try to respond to what they identify. Arrange for learners to carry out a few easy tasks in groups of two or three early in the course, which will help learners to build their confidence.

Use simple formats for examples. Make sure everyone is familiar with the basic approach before moving on to more complicated examples. If you are using your own organization's systems and forms, make sure learners have an overview of the aim of the material and where it fits in to the organization's objectives before explaining the detail. Always go through the layout and headings of a document before talking about its content. Give opportunities for people to ask questions. Learn from the group's feedback and use it to develop the format of your organization's financial reports.

Offer an enjoyable learning experience by creating a place to learn with an atmosphere that is calm and yet fun, and that makes people want to learn. Use games, quizzes, and activities. Balance the times when there is more serious content with lighter material. Having fun together make the event a memorable experience and learning messages are more likely to stick.

Allow learners time to reflect on what they already do, and if working with a group, make sure that you allow them to share their experiences and existing skills with each other and with you. Much learning takes place by confirming that what people already do is the right way to do it. Additional learning can be easily be added to what they know if learners feel that they are already almost there. Keep encouraging people and so help them to build their confidence in what they are trying to achieve.

For larger groups it is important to design a number of tasks in each activity for those who find learning more difficult, and those who need to have a more challenging task to complete while others are finishing. Use Appendix B: Explaining Financial Words to help you think through how best to explain finance terminology. When facilitating a training workshop, use the good practice suggested by Cammack (2007):

Do:

- prepare thoroughly;
- be realistic about what is possible in the time available;
- state the purpose of each session;
- deliver financial training with energy and enthusiasm;
- start off each topic with the basics;
- follow a logical pattern;
- give out written materials to support the sessions;
- let the learners do things – don't talk for too long;
- ask and invite questions;
- encourage learners – be positive;
- use a variety of methods – and have fun!

Don't:

- try to guess what the group already knows – if unsure, ask them;
- use technical words unless you first explain them;
- rush the presentation;
- try to cover everything;
- make a learner feel that he or she has failed.

Who to train and what to include

Who to train

There are a wide variety of individuals and groups who benefit from financial management training. In not-for-profit organizations these include: partner organization staff, members of community groups, non-finance staff including programme staff and fundraisers, finance staff, volunteers, the chair, treasurer, secretary, and other members of the management committee, and senior managers.

Make sure that financial courses are open to all parts of the organizations and communities with which you work. Most people need support and training to help them become confident with financial management skills. These are important skills to learn, not only to empower people and benefit organizations and communities, but to help them achieve their full potential.

Some organizations and communities send two people to external financial training sessions, for example, the chair of the management committee and the treasurer, or the manager and the finance officer. Both benefit from sharing the experience together and it is helpful to provide continuity if one of them later leaves the organization.

Topics to include

The topics included in different training and learning courses may be similar but often with a different emphasis. For example partner organizations or programme staff may learn how to prepare a budget; whereas managers and member of a management committee may need to know how to monitor and interpret a budget report. Facilitating each type of event will have different challenges, and it will depend on the TNA to identify precisely what is included. Always give opportunities to individuals and groups to say what they want to include:

Induction training. New staff usually need training in the organizational methods of financial management. This may be about issues such as claiming expenses, completing monthly documents, ordering and approving expenditure. Ideally this training will take place when the learners have got a little used to the organization and know the questions to ask. However, new members of staff sometimes need a one-to-one session soon after they arrive.

Sector-specific training. New finance (and other) staff may not have previously worked in a not-for profit organization.

The culture they experience may feel quite different, and it is important for everyone that they feel settled quickly. Issues such as gender equality and community development may be new. It is essential that finance staff become familiar with organizational priorities as soon as possible.

Financial management for non-financial managers. Managers are likely to need input on topics such as what is financial management, budgeting and cash flow, interpreting financial information, internal financial controls, and managing audits. They may also need sessions on areas connected with donor reporting, and on more specific accounting and financial management tasks.

Financial management for senior managers. Training for senior managers could include the same topics as for non-financial managers, but also areas of strategic financial management such as managing reserves, core costs, and creating a sustainable financial management strategy. They may also need input on developing finance and management controls and how to monitor these effectively.

Senior managers who struggle to understand their financial management role may be reluctant to attend a training course for fear of losing face. If they have been responsible for approving financial documents for some time, it may be hard to admit in front of others that there are parts that they do not really understand. However they still need strong financial management skills for informed decision-making. At worst this lack of skills can mean that donors lose confidence in their organization.

Confidential tutoring can help when this need is recognized. An outside tutor can provide the basics in a few private sessions and sometimes then act as the manager's ongoing mentor.

Members of the management committee. Management committee members are often busy people and not easily available to attend training and learning courses. It is important to prioritize material for these groups to fit their available time. It is sometimes possible to include some input as part of the management committee's regular meeting. Members may also need help with strategic financial management, how to interpret budgets and any other financial reports, and in identifying their financial responsibilities.

Finance staff. All of the topics listed above may also be needed for finance staff, possibly with a different emphasis. Training and learning in technical accounting topics may need to be from an external source and it is worth checking what is available locally. Donors will sometimes facilitate and fund training for groups of their partners, and it is worth talking with them in detail about possible training for finance and other staff.

It is crucial that finance staff can communicate with others in their organization. Specialist communication courses are available, and ideally need to be specifically for finance people working in the not-for-profit sector. The ideas in this book are a good starting point.

Training financial trainers. People with financial skills do not always have the skills to train others. It is important therefore to identify those who have the potential, and invest in their training to develop this role. These skills are valuable within the organization and when working with partner groups. Courses need to show how to train with an interactive approach. Specialist training of trainer courses are available for not-for-profit sector finance staff.

After the training

After the training courses it is good practice for the facilitator to include some follow-up with learners. This is important when working with small partner organizations and communities who may have just one person who is responsible for financial matters.

For example, a workshop about accounting record keeping for partners, might be followed up with a visit to the learner in their place of work to give individual advice, perhaps a few weeks after the course. This follow-up may then lead to further visits, and sometimes the facilitator acting as a mentor to the learner.

This kind of follow-up can have greater impact than the course alone, as it makes sure that the learning is fully integrated. It can be expensive but some large organizations or donors may be willing to fund follow-up activities.

To maximize the learning it is good practice to require each learner to report back to their own team or organization when they return. This can be a written or verbal report about the highlights of the event. If possible, learning materials could be copied (if copyright rules allow) for others to see. To encourage this practice it is good for facilitators to include the question 'how will you pass on this learning to others?' on course evaluation forms.

Training and learning across cultures

When facilitating training and learning courses outside your own culture, try to find out as much as possible about the culture beforehand. Keep an open mind and allow time when delivering the training to adapt or amend the materials you have prepared, if this is necessary. Look through the specific points on communicating cross-culturally in Chapters 3 and 4.

Make your role clear. Tell learners if it is all right to ask questions, as this may not be their usual way. Encourage those who are not so confident with the language of the training; use lots of small group work, and paired activities where (if necessary) people can talk in their first language, and those with stronger language skills can explain things to the others.

Use a variety of methods to keep people's interest. Make use of games to put serious topics across and to energize the learners. People from most cultures will enjoy fun activities. Avoid games that need physical contact as this may not be culturally appropriate. Choose activities that will suit people of all physical abilities and ages. Aim never to leave anyone out of the group.

Always be careful with the speed of talking if the facilitator is using his or her first language and the learners are not. Try not to use unfamiliar, long, or difficult words; avoid slang or idioms (see page 35); and also make sure other speakers speak slowly and clearly enough for everyone to understand. When giving instructions, repeat them in different ways, and check that they are understood before starting an activity.

Arrange for translators to be available if necessary, or for someone to explain complicated ideas more fully in a better-understood language. Be careful to choose translators who will translate what is said clearly and accurately and not take the opportunity to add their own material. It is sometimes useful to have a translator who knows something about the subject area. Using translators takes up valuable training time, and you will be able to cover less material as a result.

CHAPTER 9

Reviewing your organization's financial communication

This chapter aims to bring together some of the issues identified throughout this book to help you think about your situation. It invites you to review your ways of communicating financial management, involving all your stakeholders. It aims to raise standards within your organization by developing a financial communication strategy.

Questions for stakeholders

Here are some questions to ask your stakeholders. Try to encourage them to give you as much detail as possible:

Management committee and staff board

- How confident are you about dealing with the financial information you receive?
- How clear is written and verbal information at your meetings?
- What improvements could be made to the financial documents you receive?
- What further training would help you to understand the financial information better?

Senior management

- Who provides you with financial management advice?
- How useful is the financial advice you receive?
- What improvements could be made to the financial documents you receive?
- How could you improve relationships between finance and non-finance staff?

Finance staff

- How could financial skills be used to improve the impact of your organization's activities?
- What finance skills do you have that are not being fully used within your organization?
- How often have you visited one of your organization's programme activities?
- How confident are you about communicating financial information to non-finance people?

Non-finance staff

- How could financial skills be used to improve the impact of your organization's activities?
- How confident are you about using and interpreting financial information?
- What additional financial training would help you do your job better?
- What changes in financial information and/or systems could make your job easier?

Fundraisers

- What additional support would you like from finance staff?
- How confident are you in explaining your organization's financial information to donors?
- What financial training would help you to do your job better?
- What changes in financial information and/or systems could make your job easier?

Partner organizations, community groups, and service users

- How do your donors give you information about how they spend their money?
- How could you keep your community groups/users better informed about how you spend your money on their behalf?
- How confident are you at talking with donors/community groups about money?
- What improvements in your financial management would you like to make?

Donors

- How could we improve the financial information we present to you?
- How could we improve our communication with you about financial management?
- What support could you provide to strengthen our financial management systems?
- How could better financial management help our activities to have more impact?

Question any other individuals or groups you think would want to comment and list where improvements could be made. Some suggestions can be implemented easily; some may result in you saving money; others may need money. Think through what the benefit of new initiatives would be, and whether or not you need to talk with other local organizations about sharing each other's expertise, and with donors about possible funding.

Starting points

Here are a few themes from this book that could be used to improve financial management communication:

- *Provide information.* Make sure people who use financial management information and systems can see the information that they need. Circulate useful articles, glossaries of financial words, and websites. Start a central resource of written information for everyone. Make sure it is available to all and not kept in someone's office. Smaller organizations can often include the resources needed in a donor funding proposal.
- *Training and learning.* Make sure members of the management committee, staff, and others have the skills to perform the financial aspects of their jobs. If they do not, provide training in basic financial skills or find out what other training is available. Encourage finance and other staff who need to communicate financial management to seek training in communication skills. Provide

confidential training for senior staff who might otherwise lose face.

- *Cross-cultural communication.* Encourage those working with international organizations, or in other cross-cultural situations, to find out about the cultures with which they interact. Remember that cultural groups can differ within a country, organization, and even within an office. Have resources available so people can learn more, and arrange for talks from those with more experience of other cultures that you work with.

- *Recognize that good communication can improve programme effectiveness.* Encourage staff in both finance and non-finance teams to work closely and learn from each other. Recognize that when improvements are made they can have a direct result on the quality of programme work.

Financial communications strategy

For larger organizations and those based in different locations, a financial communications strategy is a way of deciding what you want staff to communicate, and how they should do it. Here is a format, based on some of the ideas in this book:

- *Identify the financial communication challenges.* Take an honest look at the communication strengths and weaknesses of the finance team, other staff and stakeholders, and your organization itself.

- *Identify where you want to be.* Build on your strengths. Recognize the weaknesses you need to address. Determine what your organization would look like if financial communication was of a high standard, and the difference that it would make to your efficiency, and the effectiveness of your programme activities.

- *Plan how to move to where you want to be.* The following steps may help:
  - Build relationships – find organizational ways of achieving this. Recognize the different cultures within your own organizations – individual and departmental. Arrange regular meetings for individual

finance and non-finance staff to look at budget reports. Examine how to develop financial communication with management board members, donors, partner organizations, and other stakeholders. Look at where finance and non-finance teams' desks are in relation to each other; encourage staff from different departments to meet informally at work-based social activities.

* Encourage staff to understand differences in international culture. Encourage people to talk face-to-face or by telephone, rather than just by email. Ask whether finance people can visit and experience programme activities. Have information available about possible cultural differences within your international team – ask those with experience to explain about ways of working with each other and to understand each other's thinking about deadlines and priorities.

* Help finance people to become service orientated and find ways to adjust to organizational cultural differences between finance and non-finance people. Find ways of identifying what non-finance staff and finance staff need from each other. Invest in developing systems to improve communication. Discourage use of technical words. Recognize how you want individuals to think and act differently. Provide training to encourage this.

* Make sure regular communications are written in plain language and that financial information is presented in a way that non-finance people can understand.

* Look at the standard emails, letters and financial documents that are circulated. Ask whether those receiving them can understand them and what their needs are. Could they be made clearer, less technical, or more user-friendly? How necessary is all the information included – could it be reduced?

• *Regularly review your financial communications strategy.* Learn as you go. As you find better ways to work make sure the strategy is updated.

Celebrate good practice

When you see good practice, celebrate it. Make sure others know and learn from it too. Encourage your organization to be learning all the time. This is the beginning of a process that will continue to develop. This bridge-building process of communicating more effectively about financial issues is a means to an end. The end is having a greater impact on the organization's own programmes and the communities they support.

References

Cammack, J. (2005) 'Exploring the effectiveness of international development NGOs' communication about finance: strategies for improvement', unpublished research, with summary at: www.johncammack.net (click on 'research').

Cammack, J. (2007) *Building Capacity through Financial Management: A Practical Guide*, Oxfam Publishing, Oxford.

Fowler, A. (1997) *Striking a Balance: A Guide to the Effectiveness of Non-governmental Organizations in International Development*, Earthscan Publications, London.

Fuglesang, A. (1982) *About Understanding: Ideas and Observations on Cross-Cultural Communication*, Dag Hammarskjöld Foundation, Uppsala.

Hall, E. T. (1989) *Beyond Culture*, Anchor Books, New York.

Handy, C. (1985) *Gods of Management*, Pan Books, London.

Munter, M. (1993) 'Cross-cultural communications for managers', *Business Horizons*, May–June: 69–78.

Oppenheimer, D. M. (2006) 'Consequences of erudite vernacular utilized irrespective of necessity: Problems with using long words needlessly', *Journal of Applied Cognitive Psychology* 20: 139–56.

Thomas, K. and Mellon, T. (1995) *Planning for Training and Development: A Guide to Analysing Needs*, Save the Children, London.

Appendix A Financial communication self-assessment

This self-assessment helps you to review your strengths and weaknesses in communicating about financial issues. Look through each of the statements and circle the score that best describes how you behave in that situation. Be as honest as you can in your scoring. You may wish to ask a trusted colleague or someone you communicate with to give you their insights, in confidence. If you are not currently involved with the issue in the statement, give yourself a score to represent how you might do it or have done in the past.

Score: 1 = Always; 2 = Often; 3 = Sometimes; 4 = Rarely; 5 = Never

Statement	Score	How can I develop my skills?
Finance and non-finance communication		
If people look at me blankly when I talk about financial issues, I stop and ask them a question	1 2 3 4 5	
I explain technical words that the other person may not understand before I use them	1 2 3 4 5	
Other people consider me to be an approachable person	1 2 3 4 5	
I try to build strong working relationships with those I need to communicate financial information to	1 2 3 4 5	
Cross-cultural communication		
I vary my communication style depending on the person receiving it	1 2 3 4 5	
I use personal greetings, such as 'how are you' when speaking to someone and communicating by telephone and in writing	1 2 3 4 5	
I try to be encouraging to those I communicate with	1 2 3 4 5	
I like to find out something about other people's cultures	1 2 3 4 5	
Written communication		
When sending an email I reread it before pressing the send button	1 2 3 4 5	
If designing a document that others will use I ask for their comments	1 2 3 4 5	
I like to talk in person as well as using email, when possible	1 2 3 4 5	
I make an effort when writing to only use words I know the reader will understand	1 2 3 4 5	

Statement	Score	How can I develop my skills?
Numeric communication		
I ask the user of numeric information how the format could be improved to make it easier to read	1 2 3 4 5	
I write/encourage others to write explanatory notes to explain budget information by those responsible for the budget	1 2 3 4 5	
I change headings and abbreviations in documents that readers may not easily understand	1 2 3 4 5	
I try to keep numeric information on one page for those just needing a summary	1 2 3 4 5	
Presenting information to stakeholders		
I use visual presentations such as pie charts to explain the figures	1 2 3 4 5	
I ask those who I present information to whether it makes sense and give them opportunities to ask questions	1 2 3 4 5	
I have a chance to visit my organization's programme activities	1 2 3 4 5	
I look at the information I present to stakeholders from their point of view before I meet them	1 2 3 4 5	
Totals		
TOTAL SCORE		

What the scores suggest and how to develop your skills

At the end add up your scores in each column. Then add up the totals to give you a total score. The lower the score the better you already are at communicating. See how well you communicate and how you might develop your skills. For each statement identify one action you could take to help develop your skills.

1–25 You are an excellent communicator. Try to develop any areas where you are not so strong; but above all keep going and try to become even better. Encourage and inspire others to improve their communication too.

25–50 You are a good communicator. There are some areas where your scores need improving. Try to work on these to become better. Encourage others to improve too.

50–75 You have identified the areas where improvements are needed. Work on the questions showing higher scores you have and use the material in this book to see where you can improve. Start by using one or two of the techniques and when satisfied with these find some more.

75–100 You have identified areas where you need to improve your communication skills. Excellent! This book is written to help you.

Start with your highest scores and identify the chapters that would be most use. Go through the suggestions and work on one or two at a time. You can learn the skills needed. Try to observe what people do who you consider to be good communicators.

Appendix B Explaining financial words

Non-finance people often find the following words difficult to understand. We can improve communication by giving clear explanations. These notes are offered to start you off. Develop them and find suitable examples for your group.

When explaining, keep asking if there are any questions and comments. Also ask questions to see if your explanation is fully understood. Be prepared to start again if necessary.

[Tips for explaining the financial words are put in square brackets.]

Accruals and prepayments

Accounting is based on the idea that we take a fixed period of time to compare our income and expenditure. We want to show 12 months' income and 12 months' expenditure and so compare 'like with like' in a financial year. If, for example, we showed 14 months income and only 10 months expenditure, the information would be misleading.

The practical way to achieve this is by 'adjusting' the amounts that have been received and paid, so it represents 12 months more accurately. Let's look at an example.

Payments in arrears [Draw the diagram on page 104 as you talk]

Imagine our year is from January to December. We should pay $120,000 a year for rent at $10,000 for each month. However, in January, we pay only 10 months' rent; that's $100,000 ($10,000 x 10 months) for the period January to October.

When we put the accounts together at the end of December, we could include just the $100,000 paid. If we did that, it would mean that our income for 12 months would not be comparable with the expenditure for rent which would only be for 10 months.

Instead accountants add the $20,000 for November and December's rent that we should have paid (and probably will pay the following January). In accounting language we call this $20,000 an *accruals adjustment*. This means we then have 12 months' expenditure for rent to compare with 12 months' income. This is represented in Figure A.1.

Figure A.1 Example of accruals adjustment

[Ask for any comments or questions. Someone may ask if this is legal. Explain that it is the standard way of comparing 'like with like' in accounting.]

Payments in advance *[Draw the diagram on page 105 as you talk]*

Let's imagine that another time we pay the rent in advance. The year is January to December again. This time we pay 15 months' rent, that's $150,000 ($10,000 x 15), in January. This covers the period from January to March of the second year.

When we put the accounts together at the end of December, we could include the full $150,000 that has been paid. However if we did, we would include some of the following year's rent in this year. Instead we include only the $120,000 that should be paid, and take off the additional $30,000. In accounting language we call this $30,000 a *prepayment adjustment* (see Figure A.2).

Figure A.2 Example of prepayment adjustment

[Ask for comments or questions.]

Annual accounts. In the annual accounts we then include the total annual expenditure figure for rent as $120,000 (this is the same whether we have made an accruals or prepayment adjustment).

We show elsewhere in the accounts that accruals and prepayments adjustments have been made. There is a note with the accounts to say they have been prepared *on an accruals basis* (a shorthand phrase meaning accruals and prepayments have been adjusted).

Does every organization adjust for accruals and prepayments? Small organizations do not usually adjust, but rather include cash and bank amounts without any adjustment. This is referred to as *cash accounting.* The disadvantage of this is that the figures do not show a 'like with like' comparison and so are less useful. Larger organizations usually adjust for accruals and prepayments. In some countries it is a legal requirement for an organization to prepare their accounts in this way.

Assets and liabilities

Assets

These are items that an organization *owns. [Ask what assets the organization you are in owns.]* The physical items such as buildings, vehicles, computers, and furniture, we call *fixed assets*, as they are items that are likely to be there ('fixed') for one year or more.

Assets also include items we *own* for a shorter period of time. For example, our bank account. The bank account is an asset, although the amount of money in it will change from day to day. Items such as this are known as *current assets*. Other current assets include the money owing to us – we call these debtors or receivables (see Debtors and creditors, below); and items that we have in stock, that we will use or sell in the coming weeks. For example, this could include booklets that we sell to service users.

Liabilities

This is money that an organization *owes*. It might be an amount outstanding that we owe to a supplier, such as electricity, water, or telephone bills that have not been paid yet. We call these creditors or payables (see Debtors and creditors, below). If we had a bank overdraft this would also be shown as owing to the bank. Together we call these items *current liabilities*.

There can also be *long-term liabilities*, which will be owed but not due to be paid until at least a year from now. These might include a long-term loan that is due for repayment in two years' time.

To develop further

We could include all the assets owned that will last for more than a year as *fixed assets*. However there may be lots of these items. So when we record them we often only include the more expensive items as fixed assets. Most organizations will decide on an amount below which assets will be treated as expenditure, for example, for items worth less than the equivalent of $500. *[Say what your organization's amount is.]* This means a small item, for example, a waste paper bin is treated as an expense rather than an asset, even though it may last for more than a year (see also Depreciation, below).

Balance brought forward and balance carried forward

Balance carried forward

This is the amount of money remaining at the end of an accounting period, which is moved ('carried forward') to the next period. It is sometimes called the 'closing balance'.

For example, our bank account has $1,000.00 remaining at the end of 31 December, the end of our financial year. This amount (or 'balance carried forward') is the same amount ('balance brought forward') shown at the start of the new year on 1 January, the next day.

Balance brought forward

This is an amount moved from a previous accounting period to start off a new period ('brought forward'). It is sometimes called the 'opening balance'.

Bank reconciliation

This is a way to agree your organization's accounting records with the bank statement (or bank pass book).

Make a link to personal bank accounts – agreeing our records with the bank is similar to what happens if we have a personal bank account. *[Ask why the amount in our bank account may be different to what the bank shows on our statement? People are likely to answer: because cheques have been written but not charged to the bank account yet, bank charges are on the statement and we did not know, direct debits or standing orders have been charged to the bank account, or money we have paid into the account has not yet appeared on the statement. Link this to what this means for our personal finances. For example, if a cheque amount has not yet been included on the bank statement, we should not spend the money because it will soon disappear, even though the bank says it is there.]*

For our personal accounts we can usually remember what the differences are likely to be. In an organization there are so many differences that we need to list them. We call this list a 'bank reconciliation statement'.

[This explanation may be enough. However, if helpful, show the example in Box A.1, or better still one from your organization, and go through it line by line.]

Box A.1 Example of a bank reconciliation statement as at 31 March

	Amount	Total amount
	$	$
Bank balance at 31 March (from bank statement)		22,646 [A]
Less: cheques not yet included on the bank statement:		
Cheque number 326001	5,845	
Cheque number 326003	7,820	13,665 [B total of cheques]
		8,981 [A–B]
Plus: items paid in but not yet included on the bank statement:		
paying-in reference 19 March		50,000 [C]
Balance in organization's own record 31 March		58,981 [A–B+C]

By preparing the bank reconciliation statement we have then identified the reason for any differences between our records and the bank's records. It helps us to keep good financial control and needs to be completed monthly, or each time we receive a bank statement.

Cash flow and cash flow forecast

We sometimes use the term 'cash flow' about our own money. Cash flow describes how money comes into and goes out of (flows through) our organizations.

[Say that we all know about managing cash flow from our personal finances. Ask 'What would you do with your own money if you did not have enough to pay for something you wanted to buy?'. You may receive answers such as 'borrow money from the bank', 'wait and buy it when I had the money', 'ask someone who owes me money to pay earlier', or 'borrow from a friend'. Say that these are the same approaches that organizations use.] Cash flow describes how money flows into and out of an organization. It is all about 'real money'. Here we use the term cash to mean the physical notes and coins, as well as the money held in our bank account.

Why is it important?

How the money moves around an organization, and crucially how much is left at any point in time, helps us see if we have enough to pay our bills as they become due. This is the same for our personal finances.

If we don't have enough money and we need to pay someone, we might be able to wait until more money arrives, or at worst our organization may have to close.

How do we manage our cash flow?

For most individuals the number of financial transactions is quite small. We can usually remember them and have a good idea of how much money we have left.

For organizations there may be hundreds or even thousands of transactions, so we need to write them down. The document we use to estimate how much money we will have is called a 'cash flow forecast'. This document helps us to plan when income will be received and payments made, and what we have left.

The cash flow forecast helps us to calculate if we can afford to make a payment at a particular time, whether we should wait until more income is received or whether we should delay payments and/or try to receive income sooner (for example by talking to donors, or giving discounts to those who owe us money to encourage them to pay sooner).

[Show an example of a cash flow forecast. Show how you would interpret it to find the money you had left at the end of each month. Also explain how to see if any income could be received earlier, or any expenditure paid later. Say if none of these were possible you might try to arrange a temporary loan or bank overdraft.]

More information and examples of cash flow forecasts can be found at www.johncammack.net (click on 'resources').

Chart of accounts (also known as coding list or budget headings)

This is a complete list of the types of money received, paid, and held ('accounts') prepared by an organization. These accounts include the list of budget headings used in different parts of the organization, and also some of the technical accounts used only by finance people. A code (see What is coding? below) may be used for, for example, grants received, salaries paid, and travel expenses.

If so, you will need to use codes when you want a cheque to be written. They say which budget the expenditure will come from. You may also see them shown on budget reports.

What is coding?

When a financial system is computerized it is likely that each account or budget will be given a unique code made up of numbers and letters, for example, ABC1234. Large organizations have many account codes. Most non-finance people only need to know those that relate to their part of the organization.

[Try not to overwhelm people by showing the whole chart of accounts if they only need a part of it. Show them the part they will use most. Ideally on no more than one page.]

Co-funding and matched funding

Co-funding

Funding for an activity from different donors. For example, 25 per cent of the total is given by three different donors, and the rest is raised locally. This other source may be the local community or another donor.

Matched funding

This is similar to co-funding, but the amount will be given by a donor *only if* an amount is raised from the other local source. The total amount that the donor gives will be exactly the same or 'matched' to the other money raised. Some donors will match the amount raised several times over (for example for every 1 rupee raised, the donor gives 3 rupees).

Core costs (also known as administrative costs, indirect costs, non-programme costs, overheads, or support costs)

These are non-programme costs for the organization. Typically they include office costs, rent, insurance, and water costs. They may also include some salaries.

Why are they important?

Not-for-profit organizations can not always claim for these as part of an activity funding proposal. If the organization is able to raise some of its own funds, then it may be able to cover some or all of the core cost. If not, it can be challenging for an organization to find enough external funding.

How do organizations fund their core costs?

There are five main strategies:

- Claim an 'administrative allowance' that some donors add to their funding for activities: this can range from 5 to 20 per cent of the funding, although often not enough to cover all the actual core costs.
- Reduce their core costs to a minimum. Most organizations have already done this, but it may help a little, although it needs to be achieved in a sensible and sustainable way.
- Use their own funds or raise funds locally: some organizations can do this, others find it difficult.
- Find a donor that specifically funds core costs: there are a few donors who will do this. For example some will fund a salary for a start-up period of a year.
- Allocate core costs to the activity budget: large organizations are likely to do this already; small organizations may find this useful, but need to stay within the donor's rules about what can be claimed. For example, it is useful to make sure items such as photocopying are charged to the activities' budget rather than the core cost budget, if copies are being made specifically for the activities.

Most organizations use a mixture of these strategies.

What do people mean by 'allocating' and 'apportioning' overheads?

Allocating overheads is an accounting technique for charging a core cost, for example the cost of the salary of someone working full-time on an activity, to the activity budget. This is done if the costs relate completely to the activity,

Organizations may also apportion costs. This could be when a core cost is partly used for the activity. For example if half of the photocopies made were for an activity, 50 per cent of the photocopying costs could be charged or apportioned to the activity budget.

Both allocating and apportioning must only be charged for expenditure that can be justified as relating to the activity.

These techniques then allow an organization to find the 'real' cost of running the activity. When these costs can be estimated, the budget including these costs can be presented to a donor. Donors may not however always agree to fund them.

[If possible find real examples that can be used.]

See also Direct and indirect costs, and Restricted, unrestricted and designated funds, below.

Debtors and creditors (or receivables and payables)

Financial words used for money owed to and owed by an organization.

Debtors

Debtors are people who owe money to an organization, possibly for goods or services provided by the organization. For example, fees owed for a training workshop that the organization provided.

Creditors

Creditors are people who are owed money by an organization. Outstanding invoices to suppliers of goods and services, for example, electricity used.

[Some countries use the words 'receivables and payables'. Receivables and payables are perhaps more descriptive and easier to understand. It is worth mentioning these words, even if not regularly used in your particular country.]

Direct and indirect costs

Together these represent the two types of costs in not-for-profit organizations.

Direct costs

For not-for-profit organizations these can relate to an activity. For example, for a training course, they are costs related to the course itself, including hire of venue, copies of materials, and the facilitator's fees and travel expenses.

Indirect costs

These are costs that cannot be traced directly to an activity. For example, for a training course these could include general advertising and publicity leaflets for all courses, and administrating the courses, such as the salary and office costs for the training administrator.

Why are these costs important?

They are important because donors will sometimes only pay for direct activity costs, and the organization itself must pay the indirect costs. This may be seen as unfair as the activity might not continue unless the indirect costs are paid. Careful attention to a donor contract is needed to see exactly what, if any, indirect costs can be also claimed. Talk with your donors about this. See also Core costs.

[If possible find real examples that can be used.]

Depreciation

This is the reduction in value of an item owned due to daily use. An example might be a vehicle that has been owned for a year and is now worth only three quarters of what was paid for it. It has lost a quarter of its original value.

When is it used?

Depreciation is calculated to show the cost of the lost value as an expense in the current year's accounts. This means when the value is shown in the accounts at the year-end, it is lower than the previous year by the amount of that year's depreciation expense.

Why is it important?

Depreciation is partly used to even out the year's expenditure. If a vehicle were bought in one year, the expenses would show a large amount in one year, even though the vehicle may be used over, for example, four years. Depreciation allows a quarter of the total amount of the vehicle to be charged as an expense for each of the four years.

Can the item be still used even though it has no value?

The accounting value of an item is to provide information for the accounts. It is an estimate. If the item is fully depreciated it may still be useable for many years. No charge will then be made in the accounts for this. It can be seen as an extra benefit at no cost to the organization.

[It is useful to have details of the organization's depreciation policy, showing the periods allowed for different types of items.]

Double-entry bookkeeping (also known as debits and credits)

This method is the technical part of accounting. Accountants need to know about double-entry, but for most purposes non-finance people do not need to know the details. Instead non-finance people just need to be able to use the information produced from that system.

Double-entry is rather like a car engine: most of us don't need to know how it works as long as we can drive and the car will take us to where we need to go.

[People often hear this term and become confused. It is better to keep the explanation as short as possible, unless they really need to know the detail. If this is not enough, say: 'so here is a brief explanation'.]

Double-entry bookkeeping

This is a method of recording transactions based on the principle that every entry is recorded in two places (double-entry). For example if we pay salaries, we need to record that salaries are paid in one part of the accounting records, and that the bank account has been reduced to pay the salaries in another part.

Debit and credit

This is the name given to each entry: one is a debit and the other a credit.

At the end of the year, accountants add up all the debit entries and all the credit entries and if everything has been entered correctly, the accounts will balance.

Double-entry bookkeeping allows you to record more complex financial information and provide detailed reports for management. These reports help an organization with its decision-making.

Imprest

This is a way of managing 'petty cash'. The person responsible for petty cash has an amount of money in cash ('the imprest'). From this they will pay for small sums of expenditure (for example, stamps, stationery).

This is often done when a part of the organization is in a different building or site to the main office. Sometimes an imprest or petty cash can mean the cash held for the whole organization.

How to manage the imprest

The amount of the imprest is agreed, for example 10,000 shillings. When the amount of money is becoming low, perhaps 2,000 shillings, more money (a top-up) is requested from the person who manages the bank account.

The person responsible for the imprest will add up the paper receipts for amounts given out so far from the imprest (in this example 8,000 shillings). When the replacement cash is exchanged for the receipts, the imprest will start all over again with 10,000 shillings. At any time the amount of these receipts and the remaining cash together should add up to the total amount of the imprest – here this would be 8,000 + 2,000 remaining cash = 10,000.

The details and amount of the receipts are written down and submitted with the receipts to justify that more money is needed.

[If you are explaining your organizational system you may wish to give people some receipts and the forms and allow them to practise the process of writing down the list and requesting a top-up.]

Reserves

Organizations sometimes save money that they don't need for their immediate requirements, in the same way as individuals do. These organizational savings are called 'reserves'.

If an organization has been in existence for some time, it may have gained a surplus (or profit) in some years, and made a deficit (or loss) in other years. The total of the previous years' surpluses, less previous years' deficits, amounts to the reserves held. They help an organization to have money available, for example, when income is not as high as was hoped, when funding is only received after an activity has been completed, or when an emergency arises.

Do we need reserves?

Some organizations have no reserves and spend all that they receive each year. Others only receive restricted funds for a particular purpose (see Restricted, unrestricted, and designated funds, below) and so cannot keep any money to build up their reserves. If the organization does not have staff, premises, or commitments they can probably manage without substantial reserves. In countries with high inflation it may not be sensible to keep hold of money, as any money saved may lose its value. However in most countries, organizations with paid staff, premises, vehicles, and commitments to their partner organizations must hold reserves to be sustainable.

Organizations need to consider what would happen if all their funding stopped. How long would it take to generate more income, and how would they survive until funding started again? A question to ask is 'how essential is it that we continue to provide the services we offer?'. If the answer is very essential, then reserves are needed.

What level of reserves?

If reserves are too high, donors may refuse to give more funding. If the reserves are too low, donors may refuse because the organization's future is uncertain. Each organization is different and the management committee needs to review what level is appropriate, based on factors such as:

- the range of donors and reliability of income sources;
- the proportion of restricted and unrestricted funds;
- outstanding commitments;
- current and future plans;
- where current reserves are – in a bank or tied up in property or investments;
- the time it would take to raise more funds;
- the amount of 'unrestricted' money raised through membership fees, donations, and local fundraising.

Reserves policy

Most organizations benefit from having a written reserves policy that states the reason for keeping reserves, the level of reserves needed, how this level will be achieved (and by when) or maintained, and how often the policy should be reviewed. Policies are usually expressed as a proportion of income, or a proportion of expenditure, or as a time period, for example '25 per cent or three months of budgeted expenditure'. Policies are approved by the management committee. Although it is good practice to have a written policy, the main benefit is that the management committee thinks through what is appropriate for their organization. Donors like to see this policy too.

Restricted, unrestricted, and designated funds

Funds given by a donor for a specific purpose (for example for the purchase of a computer), are known as 'restricted funds'. Those given for general funds with no restriction are known as 'unrestricted funds'. Donors sometimes prefer restricted funds; organizations generally prefer unrestricted funds as this gives flexibility, and helps to cover non-programme expenditure, such as core costs. See Core costs, above.

Reporting on funds

Reporting to donors is usually required for both restricted and unrestricted funds. If restricted funds can't be used for their original purpose, the organization may have to repay the money. It is however sensible to negotiate with the donor before this is necessary. If you discuss this with them in advance, donors often accept the money being used for a similar activity.

Designated funds

Another category is 'designated funds'. This is when the management committee of an organization decides to allocate some unrestricted funds for a particular purpose, for example building repairs. It is placing an internal restriction on the funds. The management committee can however 'undesignate' these funds at a later date.

A useful saying is, 'you can undesignate designated funds, but you cannot unrestrict restricted funds'.

Restricted funds are sometimes also called earmarked funds, tied funds, or ring-fenced funds. Unrestricted funds are sometimes called free funds or general purpose income.

Variance

This is a term used in budgeting to mean 'difference'. It is usually used to compare a budget amount with an actual amount of income or expenditure. The variance is the difference between the two figures.

What are 'favourable' and 'unfavourable' variances?

Favourable variances describe an actual figure that is better than the budget (that is higher than budget income, or lower than budget expenditure). Unfavourable variances describe an actual figure that is worse than the budget (that is lower than budget income or higher than budget expenditure).

[It may be helpful to show a brief real example of a budget and actual report to explain how the variance is presented in your organization.]

Voucher

This is any document that confirms an amount received or spent by the organization. An example would be a receipt written when cash was handed over, or an invoice from a supplier.

[If possible show some real examples of vouchers.]

Year to date

Organizations use a particular financial year, which could be January to December, or in some countries the government tax year is followed, for example April to March. The financial year may simply begin from the month when the organization first started.

Comparing the budget with actual income and expenditure

When budget and actual figures are compared, it is useful to review how the organization is performing over the period from the start of the financial year. So if the financial year starts in January and we are now reviewing in May, there will be five months' information. The total for the budget for this period is sometimes called 'year to date' (YTD).

[If possible find a straightforward real example that can be used.]

Appendix C Phrases in a selection of languages

Aiming for a perfect translation in any language is almost impossible! Every language can differ in how it is written and spoken, even within a small geographical area. Spellings can also vary greatly, especially if translated from a different script. The best way to accurately find phrases is to ask someone for whom this is their first language. Here is a selection to start with, but try to find and use other phrases too. It can be a great help to improving communication as most people will be delighted if you try, even if it is not quite right. If you know any improvements to these translations, please let the author know via the publishers.

Language	Greetings/hello	How are you?	Thank you (very much)	Goodbye/see you soon/ best wishes
Afrikaans*	Hallo (formal) Haai (informal)	Hoe gaan dit?	(Baie) dankie	Mooi loop Tot siens
Amharic*	Teanaste'lle'n (formal) Tadiyass (informal)	Indemin alleh? (male) Indemin allesh? (female)	(Betam) ameseginalehugn	Dähna hun (male) Dähna hungi (female)
Arabic (standard)*	As-salām 'alaykum (formal) Marḥaban (informal)	Kayfa ḥālak? (male) Kayfa ḥālik? (female)	Shukran (jazīlan)	Ma'a as-salāmah
Arabic (Egyptian)*	Is salām 'alaykum (formal) Ahlan (informal)	Izayyak? (male) Izayyik? (female)	(Mut) shakkrān	Ma'īs salāma Salām (informal)
Bengali*	Assalamualaikum (Muslim) Nomāshkār (Hindu)	Kémon achhen? (formal) Kémon achho? (informal)	Dhonnobad	Bhalo thakben (formal) Bhalo theko (informal)
Burmese*	Min ga la ba	K'amyà ne-kaùn-yéh-là? (male) Shin ne-kaùn-yéh-là? (female)	Cè-zù-bèh	Kan kaung ba zay (informal) Nauq twe dhe da paw (informal)
Chewa (Chichewa)	Moni	Muli bwanji?	Zikomo	Pitani bwino Tsalani bwino
Chinese (Mandarin)*	Nín hǎo (formal) Nǐ hǎo (informal)	Nǐ hǎo ma?	Xièxie	Zàijiàn Bàibài
Danish*	Hej	Hvordan har de det? (formal) Hvordan har du det? (informal)	(Tusind) tak	Farvel Vi ses! (informal)
Dutch*	Hallo	Hoe gaat het met u? (formal) Hoe gaat het? (informal)	Dank u	Met vriendelijke groeten (formal) Tot ziens (informal)
English	Hello (formal) Hi (informal)	How are you? (formal) How's things? (informal)	Thank you (very much)	Goodbye Best wishes

Language	Greetings/hello	How are you?	Thank you (very much)	Goodbye/see you soon/best wishes
Farsi (Persian)*	Dorood Salâm	Hale shoma chetor ast?	Mamnûnam (formal) Mersi (informal)	Bedrood Khoda hafez
French	Bonjour	(Comment) ça va?	Merci (beaucoup)	Au revoir (formal) À bientôt (informal)
German	Guten Tag (formal) Hallo (informal)	Wie geht's?	Danke (schön)	Mit freundlichem Gruss Viele Grüsse
Gujarati*	Namaste	Kem cho?	Dhanvaad	Aavjo
Hausa	Sannu	Kana lafiya? (male) Kina lafiya? (female)	Na gode	Sai an jima Sai wani lockaci (informal)
Hindi*	Namaste	Tum kaise ho (male) Tum kaisī ho (female)	Dhanyavād	Namaste Phir milenge
Indonesian (Bahasa)*	Selamat siang	Apa kabar?	Terima kasih (banyak)	Sampai jumpa lagi
Italian*	Buongiorno (formal) Ciao (informal)	Come sta? (formal) Come stai? (informal)	(Molte) grazie	Arrivederci (formal) Ciao (informal)
Khmer*	Johm riab sua Soo-as'day (informal)	Niak sohk sabaay te?	Aw kohn	Lia suhn hao-y
Nepali*	Namaste	Tapai lai kasto cha? (with respect for elders) Timi lai kasto cha?	Dhanyabad	Namaste Pheri bhetaula (informal)
Norwegian*	Goddag (formal) Hei (informal)	Hvordan har du det?	(Tusen) takk	Ha det bra (formal) Morna (informal)
Pashto*	As-salaamu' alaykum	Tsanga yee?	(Daera) manana	Da khoday pa amaan

Language	Greetings/hello	How are you?	Thank you (very much)	Goodbye/see you soon/ best wishes
Portuguese*	Olá Oi (Brazil)	Como está? (formal) Como vai? (informal)	(Muito) obrigado (male) (Muito) obrigada (female)	Adeus (formal) Até logo! (informal) Tchau (Brazil - informal)
Shona (Chishona)	Kwaziwai	Makadii?	Ndatenda Waita zvako	Muve nezuva rakanaka (informal)
Sinhala (Sinhalese)*	Aayuboovan	Kohomada?	Istuti	Naevata hamuvemu
Spanish*	Hola!	Cómo estás? Que tal?	(Muchas) gracias	Adiós (formal) Hasta luego (informal)
Swahili (KiSwahili)	Jambo	Habari yako?	Asante (sana)	Kwaheri Tuonane baadaye (informal)
Swedish	Hej (and add name)	Hur mår du?	(Stort) tack	Hej då Hälsningar (informal)
Tamil*	Vaṇakkam Alo! (informal)	Eppaḍi irukkindriirgal? Nalamaa?	(Romba) nandri	Poy vittu varugiren Apram paarkalame (informal)
Telugu*	Namaste Namaskaram	Meeru yela unnaaru?	Dhanyavaadhamulu	Namaste Shubhaṅgaa velliraṅdi
Urdu*	Assalam 'alaykum	Ap kaisi hain? (male) Ap kaise hain? (female)	(Bahut) shukriyā	Khudā hāfiz
Vietnamese*	Chào anh (male) Chào chi (female)	Anh khỏe không? (male) Chi khỏe không? (female)	Cám ón (rất nhiều)	Tạm biệt
Yoruba	Pẹlẹ o	Bawo ni	Ese (gan)	Ó dàbò (formal) Mari e laipe (informal)
Zulu (IsiZulu)	Sawubona	Unjani?	Ngiyabonga (kakhulu)	Sizobonana (informal)

*Translation based on Omniglot website: www.omniglot.com/language/phrases/index.htm Consult this website for translations into other languages.

Appendix D Wisdom on communication

He who asks questions, cannot avoid the answers.

African proverb

When the only tool is a hammer, you tend to see all problems as nails.

African proverb

Examine what is said, not him who speaks.

Arabian proverb

There's no learning without laughter from the classroom.

Aristotle, 384–22 BC

It's a terrible and tragic and counterproductive policy to avoid communicating with people who disagree with us.

Jimmy Carter, 1924–

Preservation of one's own culture does not require contempt or disrespect for other cultures.

César Chávez, 1927–93

Tell me, and I'll forget. Show me, and I may remember. Involve me, and I'll understand.

Chinese proverb

Seek first to understand, then to be understood

Stephen R. Covey, 1932–

It is greed to want to do all the talking but not to want to listen at all.

Democritus, about 460–370 BC

The most important thing in communication is hearing what isn't said.

Peter Drucker, 1909–2005

To say nothing, especially when speaking, is half the art of diplomacy.

Will Durant, 1885–1981

I never teach my pupils, I only attempt to provide the conditions in which they can learn.

Albert Einstein, 1879–1955

Make everything as simple as possible, but not simpler.

Albert Einstein, 1879–1955

We have two ears and one mouth so that we can listen twice as much as we speak.

Epictetus, 55–about 135

Communication can only register effectively when it builds on what the audience already knows.

Nick Fitzherbert

The power to question is the basis of all human progress.

Indira Gandhi, 1917–84

You cannot shake hands with a clenched fist.

Indira Gandhi, 1917–84

Whatever words we utter should be chosen with care for people will hear them and be influenced by them for good or ill.

Siddhārtha Gautama, Buddha, about 563–483 BC

There are people who, instead of listening to what is being said to them, are already listening to what they are going to say themselves.

Albert Guinon, 1863–1923

The human mind is like a parachute – it works best when it is open.

Walter Gropius, 1883–1969

Years of study have convinced me that the real job is not to understand foreign culture but to understand our own.

Edward T. Hall, 1914–2009

The essence of effective cross-cultural communication has more to do with releasing the right responses than with sending the 'right' message.

> Edward T. Hall, 1914–2009

When people talk, listen completely. Most people never listen.

> Ernest Hemingway, 1899–1961

Questioning is the door of knowledge.

> Irish proverb

One kind word can warm three winter months.

> Japanese proverb

I keep six honest serving men (they taught me all I knew): their names are What and Why and When and How and Where and Who.

> Rudyard Kipling, 1865–1936

Good communication does not mean that you have to speak in perfectly formed sentences and paragraphs. It isn't about slickness. Simple and clear go a long way.

> John Kotter, 1947–

If anyone is not willing to accept your point of view, try to see their point of view.

> Lebanese proverb

If you talk to a man in a language he understands, that goes to his head. If you talk to him in his language, that goes to his heart.

> Nelson Mandela, 1918–

You can tell whether a man is clever by his answers. You can tell whether a man is wise by his questions.

> Naguib Mahfouz, 1911–2006

Everyone may speak truly, but to speak logically, prudently, and adequately is a talent few possess.

> Michel de Montaigne, 1533–92

Communication should be clear like a mirror.

Nepalese proverb

Clear accounting maintains friendship.

Nicaraguan proverb

We don't see things as they are; we see them as we are.

Anaïs Nin, 1903–77

I know that you believe you understand what you think I said, but I am not sure you realize that what you heard is not what I meant.

Robert McCloskey, 1914–2003

We may live as brothers and sisters but straight accounting should be between us.

Pashto proverb

Speak properly, and in as few words as you can, but always plainly; for the end of speech is not ostentation, but to be understood.

William Penn, 1644–1718

The genius of communication is the ability to be both totally honest and totally kind at the same time.

John J. Powell, 1925–2009

The more elaborate our means of communication, the less we communicate.

Joseph Priestley, 1733–1804

If he who listens, listens fully, then he who listens becomes he who understands.

Ptahhotep, 25th to 24th century BC,
translated by Christian Jacq, 1947–

Do not say a little in many words but a great deal in a few.

Pythagoras, about 570–490 BC

Try to communicate with me in the way you think you understand financial issues and by this way I can help you understand these issues better.

Bryan Rambharos, 1971–

To effectively communicate, we must realize that we are all different in the way we perceive the world and use this understanding as a guide to our communication with others.

Anthony Robbins, 1960–

The single biggest problem in communication is the illusion that it has taken place.

George Bernard Shaw, 1856–1950

It's not the same to talk of bulls as to be in the bullring.

Spanish proverb

Every country has its own way of saying things. The important point is that which lies behind people's words.

Freya Stark, 1893–1993

Let a fool hold his tongue and he will pass for a sage.

Publilius Syrus, about 100 BC

Any communication ... professional needs cross-cultural research and communication skills to be able to succeed in the future.

Marye Tharp, 1931–

We should never pretend to know what we don't know, we should not feel ashamed to ask and learn from people below, and we should listen carefully to the views.

Mao Tse-tung, 1893–1976

Trust but check.

Russian proverb

If speaking is silver, then listening is gold.

Turkish proverb

Longwinded speech is exhausting. Better to stay centred.

Lao Tzu, about 600–500 BC

When the best leader's work is done, the people say, 'We did it ourselves!'

Lao Tzu, about 600–500 BC

If you wish to converse with me, define your terms.

Voltaire, 1694–1778

If I am to speak for ten minutes, I need a week for preparation; if fifteen minutes, three days; if half an hour, two days; if an hour, I am ready now.

Woodrow Wilson, 1856–1924

Think like the wise but communicate in the language of the people.

William Butler Yeats, 1865–1939

Appendix E Partnership agreements

This detailed written agreement is a basis for the financial and programme communication that follows. It can clarify possible misunderstandings, such as the need for audits and the right to undertake financial reviews and evaluations.

Key financial areas to cover include:

- the amount, currency and period of the grant and/or other support, and whether the grant will be received in full (or for example bank charges will be deducted);
- details of how and when money will be released, and what will initiate payment, for example whether it is conditional on receiving satisfactory reports;
- written or email confirmation of the transfer of the funds to the funded partner, and the receipt of funds to the funding partner;
- date when the money is to be used by, and whether amounts paid for after this deadline (for example to suppliers) for programme activities, will still be acceptable expenditure;
- when financial and activity reports must be submitted to the funding partner, for example quarterly, half yearly or annually;
- the right for the funding partner to request individual vouchers, for example, invoices and receipts;
- confirmation that all financial records will be held for at least the nationally required period (often between seven and ten years);
- any changes to the original budget to be agreed by both parties in advance, for example, changes to activities, and moving funds between budgets; limits of covering over-spendings without agreement, or items without supporting documentation;
- details of how the funding partner will assist (as needed) the funded partner with their programme management, training, and capacity-building;

- details of how the funded partner will assist (as needed) the funding partner with information about programmes;
- a copy of each partner's annual financial statements to be exchanged at the end of each financial year. For small partners this may be a basic summary;
- an audit of the partner organization, or at least the funded activity, by an approved external auditor;
- a copy of the funded partner's auditors' 'management letter' (or recommendations);
- the right of the funding partner to have an external audit of the funded activity;
- details of any final evaluation – programme and financial – required;
- whether support is likely to be renewed at the end of the current period and any conditions, and any plans for an exit strategy.

In addition details of the planned activity implementation, good governance, monitoring and evaluation, and guidelines for financial management (such as how many signatories are required for cheques drawn, and if a number of quotations are required before a capital item can be purchased) should be included. Also details of what should happen to any donated items such as vehicles and computers at the end of the partnership should be given.

It is useful to state clearly the roles and responsibilities of each partner.

Written resources

Accounting and financial management

John Cammack (2000) *Financial Management for Development: Accounting and Finance for the Non-specialist in Development Organisations*, International NGO Training and Research Centre (INTRAC), Oxford.

John Cammack (2003) *Basic Accounting for Small Groups, Second Edition with Exercises for Individual and Group Learning*, Oxfam GB, Oxford.

C. Fiennes, C. Langerman, and J. Vlahovic (2004) *Full Cost Recovery: A Guide and Toolkit on Cost Allocation*, ACEVO and New Philanthropy Capital, London.

K. N. Gupta and M. Fogla (eds) (2004) *Manual of Financial Management and Legal Regulations*, Financial Management Services Foundation, Delhi.

Kate Sayer (2007) *A Practical Guide to Financial Management*, Directory of Social Change, London.

Capacity-building

John Cammack (2007) *Building Capacity through Financial Management*, Oxfam GB, Oxford.

Bill Crooks (2003) *Capacity Self-assessment*, Tearfund, Teddington.

Deborah Eade (1997) *Capacity-Building: An Approach to People-centred Development*, Oxfam GB, Oxford.

Communication

Martin Cutts (2009) *Oxford Guide to Plain English*, Oxford University Press, Oxford.

Roger Hussey (ed.) (2005) *A Dictionary of Accounting*, Oxford University Press, Oxford.

Garry Kranz (2007) *Communicating Effectively*, HarperCollins, New York.

Cross-cultural communication

Maureen Guirdham (2005) *Communicating Across Cultures at Work*, Palgrave Macmillan, Basingstoke.

David Maranz (2001) *African Friends and Money Matters*, SIL International and International Museum of Cultures, Dallas.

Oxfam GB for the Emergency Capacity Building Project (2007) *Building Trust in Diverse Teams: The Toolkit for Emergency Response*, Oxfam GB, Oxford.

Brookes Peterson (2004) *Cultural Intelligence*, Nicholas Brealey Publishing, Boston

Craig Storti (2000) *Figuring Foreigners Out: A Practical Guide*, Nicholas Brealey Publishing, Boston.

Craig Storti (2007) *The Art of Crossing Cultures*, Nicholas Brealey Publishing, Boston.

Fundraising

Nina Botting Herbst and Michael Norton (2012) *The Complete Fundraising Handbook*, Directory of Social Change, London.

Richard Holloway (2001) *Towards Financial Self-Reliance*, Earthscan in association with Civicus and the Aga Khan Foundation, London.

Michael Norton (2009) *Worldwide Fundraiser's Handbook*, Directory of Social Change, London.

Not-for-profit management

Alan Fowler (1997) *Striking a Balance*, Earthscan, London.

Mike Hudson (2009) *Managing Without Profit*, Directory of Social Change, London.

Training

Alison Barty and Colin Lago (2003) *Working with International Students: A Cross Cultural Training Manual*, UKISA: UK Council for International Student Affairs, London.

Robert Chambers (2002) *Participatory Workshops*, Earthscan, London.

Irene Guijt, Jules N. Pretty, Ian Scoones, and John Thompson (1995) *Participatory Learning and Action – a Trainer's Guide*, International Institute of Environment and Development, London.

Lead International (2004) *Training Across Cultures: A Handbook for Trainers and Facilitators Working Around the World*, Lead International, London.

Web resources

Accounting and financial management

www.bond.org.uk (click on 'training'/'learning resources') Bond 'How to...' guides on project budgeting and other topics.

www.civicus.org (click on 'news and resources'/'toolkits') Civicus 'toolkits' include finance topics.

www.fme-online.org Financial management for emergencies.

www.johncammack.net (click on 'links' and 'resources') Links to sites about accounting and financial management, and templates for budgeting.

www.mango.org.uk Accounting and financial resources.

www.ncvo-vol.org.uk (click on 'advice and support'/'funding and finance') Resources about financial management and funding.

www.ngomanager.org (click on 'library'/'e-library') Resources on managing finance.

Communication

www.plainenglish.co.uk Good practice in writing plain English.

www.civicus.org (click on 'news and resources'/'toolkits') Civicus 'toolkits' on communication.

www.comminit.com Advice on communication.

www.communicaid.com (click on 'access point'/'PDF library') Information about culture and doing business in a range of different countries.

www.johncammack.net (click on 'research') Summary of research into financial communication in NGOs.

www.mindtools.com (click on 'communication skills') Mind tools resources, including listening.

www.ngomanager.org (click on 'library'/'e-library') Resources on communication.

www.omniglot.com A number of phrases – written and spoken – in many world languages.

Training

www.ica-sae.org (click on 'training the trainer resource pack'/'new translations') International Council on Archives; training the trainer resource pack includes information on writing learning objectives.

www.trainingzone.co.uk   Tips on a range of training topics.